Interfaith Encounter

The Twin Tracks of Theology and Dialogue

Alan Race

scm press

To my friends in the interfaith
movement across the world

© Alan Race 2001

British Library Cataloguing in Publication data

A catalogue record of this book is available
from the British Library

0 334 02843 4

First published in 2001 by SCM Press
9–17 St Albans Place London N1 0NX

SCM Press is a division of
SCM-Canterbury Press Ltd

Typeset by Regent Typesetting
and printed in Great Britain by
Biddles Ltd, Guildford and King's Lynn

Contents

Introduction

All religions traditionally provide human beings with a comprehensive orientation in life, a map for living in what Wilfred Cantwell Smith has termed our 'not quite inscrutable universe'.[1] In this sense, the religions can be described as self-sufficient: basic beliefs, ethical values, social relationships, attitudes to nature – the whole gamut of human needs and aspirations – can be catered for within a single frame of reference. There is little need to look beyond the boundaries of one's inherited religious tradition. The frameworks may be different – sometimes radically so. But the all-encompassing nature of worldview is the same.

That was yesterday. Today is different. Tomorrow may be different again. In today's global environment, self-sufficiency in religious allegiance is being eroded by an accumulation of influences. Not least among those factors is the sheer encounter with religious difference. Impressive spirituality beyond the confines of one's own inherited framework brings this home to us. It is a point raised most powerfully in the novel *The Book of Lights*, by the Jewish writer, Chaim Potok. In this story, the intellectual hero of the book, Gershon, forgoes an academic career and becomes a Jewish chaplain in the American army. On a visit to Japan, during the time of the Korean war in the 1950s, Gershon ponders the alienation he feels in the midst of a foreign culture, and engages his companion in the following reflection:

> I was taught when I grew up that the Jewish religion made a fundamental difference to the world. You know what I mean. Well, more than half the world is on this side of the planet. They don't know what Judaism is, and they're perfectly and marvelously content without it. This is a rich culture, proba-

bly no more violent and cruel than our own. Do you think
Christianity has made a big dent here?[2]

The problem for a religious understanding which clings to self-
sufficiency is how to explain the impressive fruits of religious
commitment that are manifest, often in strange guises, elsewhere.

Perhaps it is to be expected that a 'not quite inscrutable universe' would yield many different ways of coping with its questions and demands. Be that as it may, part of the many-sided
context for the next stage of Christian existence is wrestling with
the meaning of a plurality of religious interpretations of human
experience. The age-old problem of 'the One and the Many' is
being faced anew.

The Catholic theologian, Edward Schillebeeckx, sums up the
new mood for us: 'Logically and practically, multiplicity now
takes priority over unity. . . the multiplicity of religions is not an
evil which needs to be removed, but rather a wealth which is to
be welcomed and enjoyed by all.'[3] Put like that, welcoming
multiplicity as a good is more a statement of hope than fact. The
conservative forces in religion are strongly resistant to change,
and at the extremes so-called religious fundamentalism is said to
be increasing everywhere and across all traditions. Also, multiplicity could imply the indiscriminate acceptance of every manifestation of religion; yet presumably not everything labelled
'religious' is acceptable, morally or intellectually. Even in a single
tradition there are arguments about what is and what is not
acceptable. There needs to be discernment.

With these cautionary warnings, this book is written with the
intuition that the basic thrust of Schillebeeckx's summation is
nevertheless correct. Christian faith of course has always lived,
in different degrees, with religious plurality and has had to
respond to it. But, if Schillebeeckx is correct, the circumstances
in which we are called to respond today are vastly different from
those of previous generations.

But how should Christians respond to the new facts of religious plurality? The Christian debate about the relevance
and impact of living in a religiously plural world has become
complex. Big-scale Christian thinkers have turned to naming
our present age in ways that reflect this complexity. Each
compares the present circumstances with what the philosopher

Karl Jaspers designated as the 'Axial Period' (800–200 BCE),[4] a period when great figures arose in different cultural milieux around the globe, providing the foundations for the transformative and transforming religious traditions we call 'the world religions'. They describe the present historical period as one of equal paradigmatic significance, using arresting language such as the 'Second Axial Period' (Ewert Cousins),[5] the 'Age of Dialogue' (Leonard Swidler),[6] the age of a 'New World Ethic' (Hans Küng),[7] or the 'Interspiritual Age' (Wayne Teasdale).[8] This big-scale perspective is sensing that a shift of seismic proportions in religious perception is underway. If this is correct, then it is clear that the religions can no longer consider themselves to be self-sufficient as ways of approaching our 'not quite inscrutable universe'.

Yet, underlying the whole debate, there is a fundamental paradox: the more we realize our growing unity as a human race, the more we bump up against our indubitable multiplicity, our riotous diversity. In the midst of a growing sense of interconnectedness we recognize our ineradicable human plurality. We exhibit our oneness on many levels of human activity – through commerce, government, scientific and technological endeavours, education, civic life and so on – yet we feel unease in the face of forces that threaten our identity or obliterate our culturally and religiously different ways of being.

This book traces our Christian responses to the tensions and ambiguities surrounding the paradoxes of religious plurality, in two ways. I call them the twin tracks of interfaith encounter.

Following the rehearsal of a number of cumulative factors that shape the contemporary context for approaching the twin tracks, *Track One* sets out some basic parameters in the debate over the Christian theology of religions. It presents this in the form of a well-known typology which I first developed in my book, *Christians and Religious Pluralism* (SCM Press, 1983). I argued there that of the three broad typological approaches – Exclusivism, Inclusivism and Pluralism – it was the latter which did most justice to the new facts and experiences of interfaith encounter. This view maintains that transcendent Ultimate Reality, though beyond human categories, is nevertheless glimpsed and experienced authentically according to different cultural religious histories, theologies and patterns of religious life. Backing this up is a critical-realist interpretation of religious language whereby our concepts and interpretations are largely metaphorical in nature and therefore orientated on Ultimate Reality in an indirect manner.

In the face of criticism, I defended the typology in an enlarged edition of the book ten years later. There are now many voices complaining that these labels are too restrictive for what is a very multilayered transitional moment in history. However, I remain convinced about the usefulness of the typology, and will demonstrate why. My observation is that many of those who distance themselves from it nearly always illustrate one of its categories in their positive proposals. My support, moreover, for the pluralist hypothesis remains steadfast, though I hope more nuanced than previously. I have retained the label 'Pluralism' as an evaluative descriptor for this hypothesis, mainly in order to distinguish it from 'plurality', which I use as a neutral phenomenological term indicating the fact of many religions.

But the shape of the debate in the Christian theology of religions (I have come to see) has been crafted in relation to a host of other theological influences, particularly from debates in Jewish–Christian relations and in the area of christology. Therefore I have set out some of these discussions alongside the basic argument for Pluralism. All of these debates are interlinked in complex ways along Track One, but I hope that by separating out the strands I can clarify some of what is at stake.

Track Two lays out the basic claim for dialogue as the main new factor influencing our responses to plurality as a whole. Its impact is growing steadily. As a result the term embraces many meanings. I seek to shed some light on this by analysing dialogue as a twofold dynamic between what I call the 'spirit' and 'theoretics' of dialogue. My argument is that the spirit of dialogue has generated its own momentum alongside the theoretics of dialogue, and that this spirit offers challenges to the theological theoretics which have scarcely as yet been taken up. We have given ourselves permission for dialogue, but dialogue itself is outstripping the theology which granted that permission in the first place. I hope that some of the confusion about dialogue – for example, whether or not one has to subscribe to a particular option in the theology of religions before embarking on the dialogical journey – can be cleared up with the application of a distinction such as this.

More than that, I have noticed that theologians switch tracks when it seems convenient to do so. Mostly they switch from Track One to Track Two when they come up against an insoluble aspect of the theological response to plurality. If the going gets tough in theology, switch to dialogue! But dialogue is a Trojan horse, and it will eventually bring about a revolution in theological understanding.

In spite of its growing endorsement, dialogue as a form of theological quest is still having to prove itself. Therefore, from within the dialogue loop, I examine some issues in the key areas of theology, ethics and spirituality. Among other questions, these rehearse the difficult balance to be struck between absolutism and relativism, and between the One and the Many in new circumstances. The theology of religions chapter defends Pluralism against its critics; the Global Ethic chapter explores the possibilities of sharing ethical common ground across the traditions; the chapter on interspirituality discusses some of the issues of convergence and sharing in relation to religious experience. These chapters swim against the tide that assumes we are wholly boxed in by our distinguishing religious languages and that our traditions are wholly incommensurable. I am more optimistic than this and consider that no human tradition needs to remain alien in the task of interpreting the wider picture of diversity and difference. Certainly there are radical categorical differences between the religions, and it would be foolish to ignore these. But the religions are to be understood for what they are – pointers to the moon, as the Buddhist might say, and not the moon itself. On the premise that the religions are, as Harry Buck has remarked, 'touchstones of reality, not boundary stones', there are grounds for thinking that the dialogical enterprise is worthwhile and that it challenges our theological narrow-mindedness.[9]

After a period of prolonged debate about the meaning of both theology of religions in Christianity and the implications of dialogue, I have noticed that many people are entering the discussion without being familiar with earlier literature. This book moves rapidly in places over its terrain, but I trust it will help to open up the shape of a debate. At the same time, it puts its own slant on the discussion, its own interpretation and selection of what seem to me to be the main points of debate. I leave the reader to decide whether or not I have been successful.

A word now about terminology. There are objections to the use of the word 'religion' as a generic term to describe what we have come to see as certain human movements in history and comprehensive ways of interpreting life. 'Religion' might imply sameness or equality where there is little or none between 'the religions'. There are objections to the word 'faith' when it is applied generically outside its Christian sense to describe the religious apprehensions and insight of other communities and traditions. 'Faith' might imply that people of other traditions are versions of *Christian* faith, secretly, or in some other way. For some, 'religion' and 'faith' are equated with a narrow conception of what it is to be religious, a narrowness associated merely with the intellectually reflective pursuit of religious meaning and truth, normally thought of as 'belief'. And there are objections to the 'inter' of many of these terms – such as 'interfaith' or 'inter-religious' – as descriptions of encounter between people from different traditions and histories. 'Inter' might be applying the already wrongly perceived sense of 'religion' or 'faith' to relations between people of different religious communities.

None of this is free from misapprehension. I have chosen to take a relaxed stance in the face of these worries. So I have used interchangeably 'interfaith' and 'interreligious', and 'faith-communities' and 'faith-traditions', and 'religions' and 'faiths'. But I hope that the context in which I use them makes clear what is intended. 'Faith' I interpret broadly as a transcendental human capacity for openness to and awareness of Reality, an openness that stretches the imagination to encompass more than our mundane apprehensions of it. 'Religion' I take to be a family resemblance concept whereby the varying dimensions of what we call 'the religions' can be seen to overlap in criss-cross patterns, such that they are capable of being grouped together in a single category without being submerged into one another as a single entity.

On the whole, I am writing as a person of critical Christian conviction, and I am seeking to apply the insights of the study of religion to the relations between Christian faith and other religions, faith-communities, faith-traditions, spiritual paths (or whatever I should be calling them). On the whole, too, I am thinking of the great historic traditions in this book – Hinduism, Buddhism, Islam, and so on. And I fully recognize there are problems about those labels too. But we have to use something.

The literature on theology of religions and dialogue is generally content to assume that the two tracks have their own logic and can happily exist side by side. It is my conviction that this assessment is too simple, mainly for the reason that much of the information and impression we gain of plurality stems from being in dialogue, if that is understood in broad relationship terms. This means that in order to do theology we need to be in dialogue with other religious identities and communities. I hope this book goes some way towards helping that process develop.

In order to give the reader a hint of the direction taken by this book, let me cite approvingly more words from Wilfred Cantwell Smith:

> Those of us who have heard of these [other patterns of faith and religious tradition] and know something of them must affirm with joy and triumph, and a sense of *Christian* delight, that the fact that God saves through those forms of faith too corroborates our Christian vision of God as active in history, redemptive, reaching out to all men (*sic*) to love and to embrace them. If it had turned out God does not care about other men and women, or was stumped and had thought up no way to save them, *then* that would have proven our Christian understanding to be wrong.[10]

Is there any reason why a Christian should not say 'Amen' to that?

Alan Race
Feast of the Epiphany 2001

Notes

1 Wilfred Cantwell Smith, 'Shall the Next Century be Secular or Religious?', *Modern Culture from a Comparative Perspective*, ed. John W. Burbidge, New York: SUNY 1997, p. 82.

2 Chaim Potok, *The Book of Lights*, London: Penguin Books 1983, p. 247.

3 Edward Schillebeeckx, *The Church: The Human Story of God*, New York: Crossroad 1990, p. 166.

4 Karl Jaspers, *The Origin and Goal of History*, trans. Michael Bullock, New Haven: Yale University Press 1953.

5 Ewert Cousins, *Christ of the 21st Century*, Rockport, MA: Element 1992.

6 Leonard Swidler (ed.), *For All Life: Toward a Universal Declaration of a Global Ethic*, Ashland, Oregon: White Cloud Press 1998.

7 Hans Küng, *Global Responsibility: In Search of a New World Ethic*, London: SCM Press 1991.

8 Wayne Teasdale, *The Mystic Heart: Discovering a Universal Spirituality in the World's Religions*, California: New World Library 1999.

9 Harry M. Buck, 'Beyond Walls, Fences, and Interreligious Dialogue', *Journal of Ecumenical Studies* 34, no. 4, Fall 1997, p. 529.

10 Wilfred Cantwell Smith, *Towards a World Theology: Faith and the Comparative History of Religion*, London and Basingstoke: Macmillan Press 1981, p. 171.

I

Approaching the Twin Tracks

The story of Christian engagement with issues of religious plurality is complex and varied. Over the long sweep of twenty centuries it is tempting to paint a picture of evolution from closed-minded triumphalism to openly tolerant generosity. But the historical facts do not correspond with this judgement. Positive and negative attitudes have prevailed in all periods of Christian history. For example, in the early centuries, most of the Church Fathers acknowledged the positive religious value not only of Judaism and the Greek philosophers but also of Indian sages, even if they simultaneously considered the Christian revelation to surpass all of them.[1] By contrast, in our own supposedly more tolerant era, there are many Christian views that remain deeply suspicious of other religions.[2]

Nevertheless, the positive and negative outlooks have not existed in equal measure in all historical periods. It is probably true to say that a major turning-point coincided with the establishment of Christian faith as the official religion of the Roman empire in the fourth century. From being a persecuted church the Christians eventually destroyed the Roman empire's pagan temples, fostered a culture of contempt for the Jews, and later went to war with Muslims. The attitudes and beliefs that spawned this behaviour derived from both Christianity's sense of its own religious absoluteness and the hellenistic (later, western) sense of its own cultural superiority and universal destiny. It was a symbiotic match, which determined the Christian approach to other religions down to the late Middle Ages and beyond.

Today, however, we are suspicious of most claims to ideological superiority, not least because of the close connection through history between religious absolutism and the use of religion for violent ends. With the dismantling of Christendom in the modern era and the rise of democratic consciousness, a changed cultural context is preparing the way for a different response to religious plurality.

The point is often made that Christian wrestling with issues of religious plurality is not new, and this is clearly the case. What is new, however, is the awareness of the extent to which cultural and historical contexts have affected the responses. As factors of cultural conditioning shape our experiencing, thinking and living, we become aware also of how changes in cultural context have given rise to different responses to religious plurality in different places and at different times in history. Therefore, it is reasonable to ask what factors are shaping our responses to plurality in the present.

I want now to highlight a number of factors, which I believe have contributed to the newness of today's context for the Christian response to other faith-traditions. All of these factors continue to be the subject of independent study in their own right, and so my treatment of them cannot be exhaustive. I rehearse them together in order to point out their cumulative effect in altering the climate for the twin tracks of interfaith encounter. However, even at the outset, I believe we should be clear that the overall impact of these factors makes it unlikely that the Christian living with and interpretation of religious plurality can repeat the same patterns as those of our forebears. Even old words in new settings acquire new meanings.

Religious Studies

Under the secular banner of studying religion without faith-conviction on the part of the student, Religious Studies has become a multidisciplinary endeavour. It employs numerous methodological specialisms, including historical, phenomenological, psychological, sociological and anthropological approaches, among others. The upshot of this mushrooming of perspectives and knowledge is that we know more about the world's multiplicity of religious life than ever before.

A lively debate over the definition of 'religion' as a category has accompanied this growth in the study of the religious lives of human cultures. Far from being viewed as systems of believing in the intellectualist sense of assent to propositional truths, 'religions' are viewed by the scholars of Religious Studies as comprehensive ways of being and living in the world. This makes it unlikely that there is an 'essence' of religion that can be abstracted from all of the ways of life that we label for convenience 'religious'. Nevertheless, there is a family resemblance between the religions, and this can be depicted in a diagrammatic form in what I term *A Cycle of Religious Life*:

Diagnostic Principle 1

Analysis of individual
and worldly ills

End Principle 4

Goal of religious
commitment

Revelatory Principle 2

Imaginative disclosure
of transcendent meaning

Recommended Practice Principle 3

Pathway of recovery/
transformation

The religions are distinct in the content of their culturally conditioned histories, belief systems and recommended spiritual and ethical practices. But they resemble one another in that they provide a comprehensive view of reality and a context for what can be termed 'transcendent vision and human transformation'. It is this distinctiveness combined with family resemblance that creates both a 'strangeness' and a 'resonance' in the relationships between the religions.

For those who approach religious multiplicity from a faith-conviction it is the tension between the 'strangeness' and the 'resonance' that lies at the heart of many interfaith encounters.

Applying this diagram to the so-called axial religions – that is, religions whose aim is to transform life rather than reinforce any existing perceived cosmic and social order – we can note four simple staging posts in the religious interpretation of the human journey:

Diagnostic Principle 1: a diagnosis of 'what is wrong' or of what hinders the attainment of authentic/fulfilled/truthful human living (e.g. sin, grasping, illusion, disobedience);

Revelatory Principle 2: a *locus* of revelatory power which is expressed through the worldly realm (e.g. a book, a person, an experience, nature) and which opens up a transcendent order of religious reference;

Recommended Practice 3: a recommended individual and corporate practice in response to the disclosure of transforming potential (e.g. worship, meditation, pursuit of ethical excellence, community organisation);

End Principle 4: a view of the eschatological goal of religious living, which involves a radically better possibility of human good than what has so far pertained in this life (e.g. *nirvana*, eternal life, *moksha*).

The diagram should be viewed as a spiral, for the 'work' of religious conviction is never-ending in this life. It also inevitably over-simplifies the complexities of religious traditions. But as a rough guide to the basic religious outlook I believe that it reflects a common structural cycle that can be observed in all religious cultures, and particularly in those which follow the axial pattern of religious existence.

For some scholars, the notion of *A Cycle of Religious Life* may awaken suspicions that the tendency towards depicting the religions generically leads to the illegitimate 'mixing up' between very different elements of belief and practice that have developed over centuries within the great religious traditions. That is a very legitimate concern, but that is not an inevitable outcome of the cyclic model. In the face of multiplicity, there is both the 'strangeness' and the 'resonance' to honour. The former is reflected in the fact that each religion with its own cycle of interpretation exhibits very different content: Christian 'eternal life', for example, is not the same as Buddhist '*nirvana*'. Yet the latter is reflected in the structural similarity, which draws the religions into relationship: *nirvana* 'resonates' with eternal life.

The scientific study of religion claims to be neutral with regard to religious commitment. Nonetheless it is indispensable to interfaith encounter for a number of reasons, which might include:

- clarifying terms and correcting misconceptions about particular faith-traditions and their historical developments
- offering scholarly challenges to assumptions and processes governing encounters between individuals and faith-communities
- assisting the intellectual critique of models that seek to honour both the 'strangeness' and the 'resonance' between traditions.[3]

In addition to these scholarly goals in the importance of Religious Studies for interfaith encounter, there are other purposes that the study of religion may usefully serve beyond the strict limits of its claim to be methodologically neutral. So Friedrich Heiler, the celebrated German historian of religion, has pointed to the role of Religious Studies in helping to lift the religions out of the pit of mutual suspicion: 'A new era will dawn upon mankind when the religions will rise to true tolerance and co-operation on behalf of mankind (*sic*). To assist in preparing the way for this era is one of the finest hopes of the scientific study of religions.'[4] Heiler has here highlighted a public role for the study of religion that is fully consonant with the concerns of the twin tracks of interfaith encounter analysed in this book.

Friendships

Religions can be said to be self-sufficient in that they provide their adherents with a comprehensive way of being, thinking and living. However, friendships between people of different traditions trespass the boundaries of religious commitment. In friendship, we learn how a religion informs another person as a way of life rather than simply as a given set of beliefs, rituals or moral prescriptions.

Interfaith encounter as friendship is also giving birth to a growing literature reflecting on the implications of new experiences. Let me illustrate this with reference to a figure from a previous generation. Charlie F. Andrews (1871–1940) was an

Anglo-Catholic Christian missionary who travelled from England to join the Cambridge Mission to Delhi in 1904 and whose life is remembered as a 'catalogue of friendship'.[5] Through friendship he learned of what he came to consider as the authentic work of God in other religious lives. In his own words:

> There is an experience which has happened to me so frequently in India that I have no longer come to look upon it as strange or unusual. It is this. Continually, when I come into new surroundings and meet with new faces, the consciousness of the presence of Christ among those I meet is borne in upon me. If one may dare to express what happens in words, it is as if I saw Christ in their faces and knew that He was present. They reveal Christ to me. This is, I am aware, mystical language; but I can express the reality in no other adequate manner.[6]

It is the sheer fact of Andrews' openness that is admirable in this passage. As a Christian he inevitably uses christological language to account for his experiences. But the point is that through the friendships Andrews developed, he was drawn into a theological quest to find an adequate language that would do justice to an unexpected experience, the explanations for which were not readily available to him in his immediate Christian tradition.

Andrews had the remarkable capacity for developing friendships with many of India's leading intellectual, social and political leaders. He was a close co-worker with Mahatma Gandhi, for example, in the struggle for India's independence from British colonial rule. An admirer and chronicler of Andrews' theological journey in India, Daniel O'Connor, has drawn attention to the 'remarkable testimony' from a Muslim scholar, Nazir Ahmad, of the 'devoted friendship' between Andrews and a fellow Muslim from Delhi, Munshi Zaaka Ullah. As Ahmad says: 'Their love for each other was pure and disinterested. Both of them had penetrated deep down in to the fundamental truth of religion itself, apart from creeds and dogmas. Their mutual affection, which was so profound and sincere, was really love for the sake of God. It did not depend on man'.[7]

We might pause at the confident possibility that both men had arrived at 'the fundamental truth of religion itself', unpopular as this type of explanation has become. Furthermore, O'Connor himself has suggested that friendships can also harbour degrees of naivety, particularly about differences between religions. It may be that, as O'Connor suggests, a degree of correction about this in the case of Andrews is required, though Andrews himself did write to Gandhi complaining of this same tendency in the great leader's public addresses.[8] Nevertheless, friendship between people for whom faith is not incidental in their lives, can bring changed perceptions about the 'religious other', and from which a different appreciation of the theological meaning of plurality springs.

The history of interfaith relations has yet to uncover much of this spirit of friendship which has perhaps done more to alter the map of interfaith reflection than has so far been appreciated. I shall take up some of the reflective issues further in Chapter 5. Through friendship, self-sufficiency in religion is turned inside out, suggesting that religious identity is not only a function of one's own stories, traditions and practices, but is also evolving to become dependent on the broader context of interfaith relationships.[9]

Mission

It may be that, as the Vatican II document *Ad Gentes* (Decree on the Missionary Activity of the Church) puts it, 'The pilgrim church is missionary by its very nature', nevertheless the story of the spread of the Christian gospel among the nations is an ambivalent one. In addition to planting churches across the globe, missionary activity has also been accused of complicity in the destruction of non-western cultures, the political and economic subjugation of colonized peoples, and the denigration of non-Christian religious commitments. Contemporary missiology, therefore, is busy trying to separate out the negative effects of missionary expansion from the positive calling and enduring aspects of Christian mission.

Partly as a result of the critique of some forms of missionary activity, there has been a major paradigm shift in the meaning of

Christian mission. No longer primarily a matter of saving souls or extending the church, the controlling theological notion has become the *missio dei*, or the Mission of God in and to the world. 'The *missio dei* is God's activity,' says the celebrated missiologist, David Bosch, 'which embraces both the church and the world, and in which the church may be privileged to participate.'[10] Although Bosch himself did not draw this conclusion, the *missio dei* opens the door for the activity and presence of God to be discovered in forms additional to those celebrated through the churches.

This broadening of the scope of mission has gathered pace through the twentieth century. Compare, for example, the optimism of the 1910 Edinburgh World Missionary Conference in its confidence about the 'evangelisation of the world in this generation' (a phrase borrowed from John Mott's book of the same title, published in 1900)[11] with the universalizing affirmation of the World Council of Churches Seventh Assembly, held in Canberra in 1991, which supported the view that 'a reconciled and renewed creation is the goal of the church's mission.'[12] In other words, through the course of the twentieth century, the theological meaning of mission has undergone a fundamental shift in the direction of universalizing the missionary presence of God through all creation. In parallel response, the churches have expanded their missionary activity in numerous directions, so that it now encompasses, in addition to traditional evangelism, at least the following: inculturation, political liberation, Christian presence, the search for justice, peace, and sustainable development, and dialogue with other religions.

In relation to the twin tracks of this book, such a major reinvention of mission leads to a different relationship with people of other religions than that associated with the traditional notion of mission, and therefore to a different Christian understanding of the place of other faith-traditions in the purposes of God. It has even been said that the *theologia religionum* (theology of religion) is the 'epitome of mission theology'.[13]

The roots of the changing perceptions of mission in relation to the world religions stem also from experiential encounter. Most missionaries travelled from Europe convinced of the superiority of the Christian message and its power for salvation. Their experience brought them face to face with a different reality. In addition to the challenging aspect of personal friendships already mentioned, Charlie F. Andrews, for example, discovered something different from what he expected in the literature of the Indian people among whom he lived:

> When we turn from the personal lives of the Indian people with whom I have lived all these years, to the literature which is regarded by them all as a part of their own sacred scriptures, I find in this also passages of such deep spiritual beauty and moral insight, that I have found myself constantly saying – 'This is nothing else than Christian'.[14]

This was the experience of a European missionary in the first half of the twentieth century. Others have documented different degrees of positive engagement with people of other religions stretching back further.[15] We have not moved from a 'wholly benighted' view of mission to a 'dialogically open' view in a single step. Nonetheless, between Edinburgh (1910) and Canberra (1991) there has been a considerable shift in missiological understanding, creating space for a new relationship between the religions and Christian reflection about those relationships.

Dialogue

In interfaith circles, dialogue has become a portmanteau expression, describing many activities and serving numerous purposes. At root, as the etymology of the term suggests, dialogue signifies communication *across* worlds of discourse and difference. Dialogue involves the critical sharing of experiences, insights and values through commitment to mutuality in the search for truth. It is most clearly a process, a bringing together of different voices without prescribing necessarily a particular outcome. Dialogue is, as Wesley Ariarajah avers, 'an attempt to help people to understand and accept the other in their "otherness"'.[16] In this sense, it shows a tendency towards valuing plurality and this explains its adoption by the interfaith movement.

Theorizing about dialogue is bound to remain controversial. At the experiential level, however, dialogue is assuming a significance as all-embracing as the new agenda of mission. For example, Roman Catholic literature is fond of pointing to four contextual arenas in the pursuit of dialogue. These were set out clearly in the document *Dialogue and Proclamation* (1991), which was composed jointly by the Pontifical Council for Inter-religious Dialogue and the Congregation for the Evangelization of Peoples:

(a) The *dialogue of life*, where people strive to live in an open and neighbourly spirit, sharing their joys and sorrows, their human problems and preoccupations.

(b) The *dialogue of action*, in which Christians and others collaborate for the integral development and liberation of people.

(c) The *dialogue of theological exchange*, where specialists seek to deepen their understanding of their respective religious heritages, and to appreciate different spiritual values.

(d) The *dialogue of religious experience*, where persons, rooted in their own religious traditions, share their spiritual riches, for instance with regard to prayer and contemplation, faith and ways of searching for God or the Absolute.[17]

This is a comprehensive statement of the forms of dialogue, the general thrust of which could easily be reflected in comparable Protestant and Orthodox literature. Given this comprehensive scope, the question is often raised about the relationship of dialogue to mission. As I pointed out in the section above, dialogue is cited as one of the facets of the many dimensions of the *Missio Dei*. Yet, as dialogue itself is also all-embracing, it is small wonder that this has led to significant tensions within Christian theology, raising acutely the question of the compatibility between the twin tracks of Christian relationships with other religions.

Many influences have fed into the rising tide of dialogue. Undoubtedly, the rise of toleration in European culture and the right to freedom of religion stemming from the human rights field, have contributed to the gradual change of climate (see below). Equally significant has been the creation and subsequent momentum of international interfaith movements committed to dialogue in its broadest sense.[18] The first Parliament of the

World's Religions, held in Chicago in 1893, embraced a number of concerns and goals. These included, at least the following:

- to promote mutual understanding between people of diverse religious traditions;
- to display the distinctive truths of the world religious traditions and the commonalities between them;
- to encourage the sharing of the spiritual resources of the religions for tackling the social and moral problems of the world;
- to devise a united front of religion (but not a single religion) against non-spiritual views of life.[19]

Many of these concerns remain high on the agenda of relationships between faith-communities, reflecting the gradual impact of the dialogue movement as a whole.

In relation to the twin tracks of interfaith relations, dialogue both stems from and bolsters plurality. No longer an optional extra, for numerous reasons it is beginning to reshape the theological and religious landscape. Over recent decades the literature dealing with dialogue has largely concentrated on discovering permission for dialogue in scripture and tradition. This will continue. But dialogue is also yielding new data and new experiences which, in turn, call for new models of theological reflection. This is the main impact of dialogue on the concerns of this book.

Critical thinking

Whatever we affirm about God is bound to be indirect. This is a commonplace yet cardinal orthodox principle in theological discourse. In the interfaith field, however, this principle carries radical implications. It entails that assertions of religious truth embodied in Christianity need not automatically rule out similar assertions in another religion. Religious language, if it depicts its object indirectly, will find an either/or approach to religious truth unsatisfactory. Comparing religions is more akin to comparing languages or civilizations than to comparing truths in any plain or direct sense.

Let me now very briefly illustrate the impact of critical thinking more concretely with reference to the use of the Bible and Christian tradition, in the context of religious multiplicity today. Inevitably, any authoritative guidance from sources cannot consist simply in repeating the formulae or approaches of the past, for critical thinking itself implies that our notions from the past will need to be revised.

It is often assumed that the Bible is 'against' other religions, and this is certainly the impression created when isolated texts are cited as evidence of the Bible's cautionary outlook. The words of Jesus in John's Gospel: 'I am the way, the truth, and the life; no-one comes to the Father except by me' (John 14.6); and Peter's words in the Acts of the Apostles: 'There is no salvation in anyone else at all, for there is no other name under heaven granted to men, by which we may receive salvation', certainly on the surface seem to settle the matter. But appeal to isolated texts is not the only use that can be made of the Bible. The broad picture is much more nuanced than that suggested by the proof-texting method. In this connection, the Reformed theologian, Richard Plantinga, speaks of the 'universal-creational' and the 'particular-revelational' moments of biblical revelation. These are related in that God's concern for the whole of creation comes to dramatic expression in the atoning work of Christ, which thereby becomes the key for 'making possible the salvation of all the world'.[20]

There is much support for this use of scripture, from both Catholic and Protestant theologians, in relation to the issues of religious plurality. However, in terms of critical thinking, even this nuanced non-literal picture may be applying an alleged biblical pattern too directly. What if our context for addressing the Christian response to religious plurality is entirely different from that of the biblical writers? Commenting on the so-called 'exclusivist' text from John's Gospel (14.6) cited above – from a Gospel often credited with balancing the 'universal' and the 'particular' presence of God in creative measure – the British New Testament scholar, John Fenton, has shown how this text becomes misleading when taken out of its first-century context:

What seems to have happened is that awareness of what they had received through faith in Christ and baptism in his name led Christians to make claims for Jesus that were total: all that they had was his gift; in this context, that was all they could say, and they could not be expected to say less. To ask whether those who are faithful to another religion, either before the birth of Christ or after, are in communion with God and partake of his Spirit, is to raise an entirely different question, and to move into a context that calls for other considerations.[21]

Fenton's point is not that John's Gospel is to be bypassed completely when responding to religious plurality, but simply that 'other considerations' necessarily enter into the equation in a later historical context. Another New Testament scholar, Heikki Räisänen, expresses this same point with relaxed clarity: 'Having an idea of where we come from may aid us in orientating ourselves to where we are now and where we wish to go, but the yield is bound to be indirect.'[22] Obviously this leaves all the work to do in connecting biblical patterns of response with 'where we wish to go'. In this hermeneutical task, a critical approach to scripture allows biblical patterns to act as stimuli for making certain avenues of enquiry in relation to plurality as this impinges on us now; it need not treat the patterns of biblical response as prescriptions for our own times. Even Plantinga's non-literal view of scriptural patterns need not be determinative for us.

When it comes to considering the role of dogmatic traditions in the Christian response to other traditions, critical thinking has deeply challenged many Christian assumptions about its own sense of religious absoluteness. Leonard Swidler summarized the overall effect of the de-absolutizing of truth and knowledge as follows: 'Where immutability, simplicity, and monologue had largely characterized our Western understanding of reality in an earlier day, in the past 150 years mutuality, relationality, and dialogue have come to be understood as constitutive elements of the very structure of human reality.'[23] If Swidler is correct in this judgement, then the 'one and only' tendency in religious faith seems unsustainable.

There may be dangers in presenting the case for the de-absolutizing of Christian truth in so forceful a manner. In particular, the mounting impression that relativism in religious knowing may be the only conclusion to draw seems debilitating. Yet there is no reason for this impression to assume overwhelming proportions. For neither a relativism which considers reality to be a function of a series of mutually impenetrable perspectives, nor one which reduces truth to local opinion or preference, necessarily follows from critical thinking. Pursuing a different route, de-absolutizing religious truth entails that the religions will present 'from below', their varying perspectives, insights and beliefs to a common enterprise, where religious truth in its fullest sense will be the fruit of encounter, exchange and dialogue.

Toleration

The origins of the notion of toleration, at least in its western European form, lay partly in the secular rejection of the wars of religion between Catholics and Protestants in the early modern period. In a secular society, religions have no need to turn to war in defence of a particular brand of theocratic rule. But the more positive reasons for toleration between the religions are reflected in the United Nations Universal Declaration of Human Rights, which states in Article 18 that: 'everyone has the right to freedom of thought, conscience, and religion . . . and to manifest his religion or belief in teaching, practice, worship, and observance'. Toleration allows in principle for faith-communities to be treated on an equal basis in a society determined largely by a secular ethos.

In one form, toleration implies 'putting up' with the one who is 'other', provided that this 'other' does not interfere in the internal affairs of 'my' community and tradition. But such a minimalist view has become unrealistic in the face of the strain that the sheer variety of religious traditions and groupings jostling for equal recognition in the civic sun, places on toleration. In a nutshell, toleration between religions, as a form of minimal acknowledgement that plurality is a fact of existence, is not enough for more complex multifaith and multicultural societies. There is a move to go 'beyond toleration'.

In Britain, for example, the case for evolving beyond toleration has been argued forcefully by the acclaimed Parekh Report, which calls for a multiethnic society based on a 'widespread commitment to certain core values: equality and fairness; dialogue and consultation; toleration, compromise and accommodation; recognition of and respect for diversity; and – by no means least – determination to confront and eliminate racism and xenophobia'.[24] In this list 'toleration' is one component part of a set of values which comes within the purview of much of the language current in interfaith relationships.

The deeper responsibilities within the notion of toleration have also been recognized in the literature of the United Nations. Thus in the 'Declaration on the Elimination of All Forms of Intolerance and of Discrimination Based on Religion or Beliefs', which was adopted by the General Assembly of the United Nations in 1981, freedom of religion was not simply declared as a goal in its own right, but was adopted as part of a wider purpose: 'freedom of religion and belief should also contribute to the attainment of the goals of world peace, social justice and friendship among peoples and to the elimination of ideologies or practices of colonialism and racial discrimination'.[25] Given the history of interreligious antagonism and the support for colonialism and racial discrimination that the religions (including Christianity) have shown in the past, the Declaration is not only tantamount to an international reprieve for religion (!) but also puts them to work for the international good in new ways.

But a paradox now opens up. As toleration for the sake of the common good draws the religions together so their distinctive structures of spirituality, ethics and belief propel them apart. Therefore any new framework of toleration that may be developed can only be open to religious perspectives in so far as those perspectives themselves are based on dialogical respect and responsible co-operation. The international community, it seems, is summoning religious communities to a reversal of many previous attitudes and practices! As the legacy of antagonism between rival religious commitments runs so deep, the religions are required more than ever to adapt themselves critically to a new spirit of toleration as a condition for shared participation in emerging multicultural and multireligious societies. The principle of toleration is expanding to encompass mutuality, shared values and the search for new ways of religious understanding and co-operation.

Interdependent world

Many of the problems that the world faces do not respect national boundaries. The threats of population increase, poverty, ecological degradation, disease, militarisation in league with a flourishing arms trade, and political instability affect every nation. They are embedded in our political and economic relationships and can hardly be ignored. Given their planetary scale, it is small wonder that some theologians and others have tried to identify the spiritual resources for tackling these global crises. It is small wonder too that such resources will likely have to derive from a sense of shared values and beliefs. Somehow the nature of the threat which ignores boundaries requires to be answered by a religious approach which is equally impatient with boundaries.

It may be difficult to speak wholly intelligibly about that sense of spiritual unity – grasped intuitively by all religious traditions – that binds together human beings, animals, and the earth itself, but such universalistic appeals readily come to the surface in the face of threats to the future of the planet. For example, the *Earth Charter*, which was first issued in 2000 CE, embodies the hope for multidisciplinary co-operation, including interreligious co-operation, on many practical and theoretical fronts for the sake of solving global problems. As the fruit of many years of inter-disciplinary consultation among scientists and scholars of the humanities, philosophy and religion across the globe, the *Earth Charter* evokes the spiritual heart of the challenges which face the world community: 'The global environment with its finite resources is a common concern of all peoples. The protection of Earth's vitality, diversity, and beauty is a sacred trust.' Echoing the call for a Global Ethic, which was first issued publicly in 1993 at the second Parliament of the World's Religions held in Chicago, USA, the *Earth Charter* goes on to appeal for 'a shared vision of basic values to provide an ethical foundation for the emerging world community'.[26]

Other international bodies have expressed similar concerns about the future of our 'one world'. For example, an UNESCO International Expert Group study of human cultures has written: 'The search for peace, for understanding, for solidarity, for unity, is ultimately a search for the harmonious co-ordination of diversity. Because both diversity and unity are culturally determined, the search is also intercultural dialogue and co-operation.'[27] 'Intercultural dialogue' is closely related to 'interreligious dialogue' for the simple reason that cultural values have largely been shaped by religious apprehensions of life; and, in spite of secularism, that still remains true for large numbers of cultural groupings. Therefore the role for dialogue between religions for the sake of the 'harmonious co-ordination of diversity' can scarcely be ignored.

Indeed, it may be that such collaborative work has already begun to prove itself. As the scholar of comparative religious ethics, Bruce Grelle, has written: 'The inter-faith movement is one of the few places in contemporary society where it is possible to employ a moral language of universal interests and the common good while recognizing and even celebrating the irreducible plurality of religious, social, and cultural life.'[28]

The language of 'global ethics' for 'the emerging world community' may at times seem inflated. So long as we remain alert to the potential dangers hidden within the language of 'globalization', particularly dangers of economic exploitation, the pressures to find ways of pursuing a sustainable future, backed by a shared ethical vision, seem inescapable. The alternative is to surrender to the prophets of doom. Grelle's endorsement of the movement for interfaith understanding and co-operation is grist to the mill for the concerns of this book.

The factors I have explored above are cumulative in their effect on any Christian consciousness which seeks to respond to the issues of religious plurality in today's interconnected world. Some of them arise, broadly speaking, from intellectual shifts within Christian thought; and some derive from external influences and changes in the cultural and political patterns of global life. Together they make a substantial difference to how we experience religious plurality today and therefore on the credibility of the response we might make. In one sense, it could be said that they are in part responsible for creating both of the tracks of interfaith encounter.

From the internal perspective of the Christian theology of

religions, shifts in the understanding of missiology and the absorption of critical thinking have opened up new channels for interpreting religious plurality and for exploring the meaning of religious truth afresh in a global environment. From an external perspective, new friendships between people of different religious backgrounds and the rise of the dialogue movement have contributed to the creation of a wealth of contact across religious barriers. Shifts in Religious Studies, the deepening demands of the notion of toleration and challenges to develop diversity-in-unity for the sake of our 'one world' future, add further weight to shaping a significantly new context for interfaith activity and reflection.

As a result of this multitude of influences, the manner in which we experience the presence and meaning of religious plurality is bound to be different from the way it has been experienced in the past. The American Christian theologian, Langdon Gilkey, has called this new experience of religious plurality the 'rough parity' between religions. Without such an estimate, believes Gilkey, 'a serious discussion of diversity and its theological meaning would not be undertaken, nor would serious and authentic dialogue between religions be possible'.[29] It is to the challenges provoked by the 'rough parity' of religions that the remaining chapters of this book are addressed.

Notes

1 Clement of Alexandria, for example, in the third century noted the positive spirituality of 'some called Sarmanae, and others Brahmins . . . Some, too, of the Indians obey the precepts of Buddha; whom, on account of his extraordinary sanctity, they have raised to divine honour' (*Stromata* I, 15), cited also by Jacques Dupuis SJ, *Toward a Christian Theology of Religious Pluralism*, Maryknoll: Orbis Press 1997, p. 68.

2 For example, the senior ecclesiastical figure, Cardinal Joseph Ratzinger, the prefect of the Vatican's Congregation for the Doctrine of the Faith, called Buddhism 'spiritual, mental autoeroticism', in an interview with the French weekly *L'Express*, March 1997. I am grateful to Wayne Teasdale, *The Mystic Heart: Discovering a Universal Spirituality in the World's Religions*, Novato, California: New World Library 1999, p. 45, for this reference.

3 See Peggy Morgan's insightful article: 'The Study of Religions and Interfaith Encounter', *Numen* 42 (2 May), pp. 156–71.

4 Cited in F. Whaling (ed.), *Contemporary Approaches to the Study of Religion*, vol. 1, Mouton 1985, p.182. I am grateful to Peggy Morgan, for this reference.

5 This example of Charlie F. Andrews is taken from Daniel O'Connor, *Relations in Religion*, India: Allied Publishers 1994.

6 *The Testimony of C. F. Andrews*, Madras: CLS 1974, introduced by Daniel O'Connor and published for The Christian Institute for the Study of Religion and Society, Bangalore.

7 O'Connor, *Relations in Religions*, p. 7.

8 In a letter from Charlie Andrews to Gandhi: 'Your talk yesterday distressed me, for its formula "all religions are equal" did not seem to correspond with history or with my own life and experience.' Cited by Daniel O'Connor in *The Testimony of C. F. Andrews*, p. 118.

9 See also S. Wesley Ariarajah, *Not Without My Neighbour: Issues in Interfaith Relations*, Geneva: WCC Publications 1999, p. 48.

10 David Bosch, *Transforming Mission: Paradigm Shifts in Theology of Mission*, Maryknoll: Orbis Books 1991, p. 391.

11 John Mott, *Evangelisation of the World in this Generation*, London: SCM Press 1900. Chapter 5 was entitled 'The Possibility of Evangelising the World in this Generation in View of Some Modern Missionary Achievements.'

12 *Come, Holy Spirit*, reproduced in James A. Scherer and Stephen B. Bevans, SVD (eds), *New Directions in Mission & Evangelisation 1*, Maryknoll: Orbis Books 1992, p. 84.

13 Bosch, *Transforming Mission*, p. 477, citing Eric J. Sharpe.

14 *The Testimony of C. F. Andrews*, p. 219.

15 See, for example, Kenneth Cracknell, *Justice, Courtesy and Love: Theologians and Missionaries Encountering World Religions 1846–1914*, London: Epworth Press 1995, for the seeds of many theological ideas which would return in the later twentieth century.

16 Ariarajah, *Not Without My Neighbour*, p. 14.

17 *Dialogue and Proclamation*, reproduced in *New Directions in Mission and Evangelization 1*, p. 187; cf. the discussion of these four areas by Donald W. Mitchell, 'A Revealing Dialogue', *Interfaith Spirituality*, The Way Supplement 78, London: The Way Publications 1993, pp. 42–53.

18 The first history of these movements has been documented by Marcus Braybrooke, *Pilgrimage of Hope: One Hundred Years of Global Interfaith Dialogue*, London: SCM Press 1992.

19 In addition to Braybrooke's history, see the evaluative essay by A. Durwood Foster, 'Current Interreligious Dialogue', *Inter-Religious Dialogue: Voices from a New Frontier*, ed. M. Darrol Bryant and Frank

Flinn, New York: Paragon House 1989, chapter 5. Also see, Marcus Braybrooke, *Faith and Interfaith in a Global Age*, London: SCM Press 1998.

20 See the Introduction to Richard J. Plantinga (ed.), *Christianity and Plurality: Classic and Contemporary Readings*, Oxford; Blackwell Publishers 1999, Part I.

21 John Fenton, *Finding the Way through John*: London: Cassell, Mowbray 1995, pp. 95f.

22 Heikki Räisänen, *Marcion, Muhammad, and the Mahatma: Exegetical Perspectives on the Encounter of Culture and Faiths*, London: SCM Press 1997, p. 15.

23 Leonard Swidler, *After the Absolute: The Dialogical Future of Religious Reflection*, Minneapolis: Augsburg Fortress Press 1990, p. 6. In chapter 1, Swidler lists six developments in philosophical epistemology which together create a new matrix for coming to know the truth of reality. These are:

(a) Historicism – historical context contributes towards shaping knowledge;
(b) Intentionality – truth is expressed in terms of the *praxis* or 'action-orientation' of the writer;
(c) Sociology of knowledge – truth is conditioned by the cultural context, gender and class of the perceiver's whole outlook;
(d) Limits of language – knowledge is partial because it is linguistically constrained;
(e) Hermeneutics – truth involves interpretation, thereby connecting subject with object in a circle;
(f) Dialogue – knowledge is relational.

24 The Runnymede Trust Commission Report, *The Future of Multi-Ethnic Britain*, London: Profile Books 2000, p. 56.

25 Cited in Joel Beversluis (ed.), *Sourcebook of the World's Religions: An Interfaith Guide to Religion and Spirituality*, Novato CA: New World Library 2000, p. 219.

26 Beversluis, *Sourcebook of the World's Religions*, pp. 303ff.

27 E. Laszlo (ed.), *The Multicultural Planet*, Oxford: Oneworld Publications 1993, p. 6.

28 Bruce Grelle, 'Scholarship and Citizenship: Comparative Religious Ethicists as Public Intellectuals', *Explorations in Global Ethics: Comparative Religious Ethics and Interreligious Dialogue*, ed. Sumner B. Twiss and Bruce Grelle, Boulder, Colorado: Westview Press 1998, p. 56.

29 The phrase 'rough parity' was launched by Langdon Gilkey in 'Plurality and Its Theological Implications', *The Myth of Christian Uniqueness: Toward a Pluralistic Theology of Religions*, ed. John Hick and Paul F. Knitter, Maryknoll: Orbis Books 1987, p. 37.

2

Track One:
Christian Theology of Religions

The Indian Christian theologian, Stanley Samartha, once asked the question: 'Can it be that it is the will of God that many religions should continue in the world?'[1] The question is rhetorical because it seems to expect the answer 'yes', with an implicit hint that such an answer might free the Christian community from its obsession with categorizing other religions as a problem. Most Christian answers to the challenges of religious diversity have explained this diversity as a function of either error or moral failure. But Samartha has opened the door to the scandalous possibility that other religions are the products of divine intention rather than human accident – with the consequence that they have a theological right to exist and be heard!

In asking his question, Samartha inevitably betrays his own Indian religious ethos, which classically celebrates diversity as the norm. But he is also responding to the full accumulative weight of the new global context. It is not only the *matter of fact existence* of many religions but also their *persistence* as vibrant contexts for 'transcendent vision and human transformation' that requires explanation. Can there be more than one revelation of Ultimate Reality, on the same human level, as it were, as Christianity?

Formulating the question of plurality in this manner opens up the central question of the meaning of revelation. By revelation I refer to the dynamic tension in religious apprehension between, on the one hand, the particular experience of transcendent vision that has been generated initially under specific cultural and local circumstances, and on the other hand, the universal power and presence of transcendent vision that is accepted as the prior ground of its local manifestation. There is a theological tension between the two: the apprehension of divine universal presence derives from the power of particular experience and the particularity of experience serves a universal purpose. Negotiating this theological tension becomes more complex once the contemporary plural context is viewed positively.

This chapter rehearses in broad terms some of the theories currently discussed under the heading of the Christian theology of religions. It will follow a typology which I first developed in 1983 under the much-discussed categories of 'Exclusivism', Inclusivism' and 'Pluralism'. Since then, the typology has been criticized as being either too simplistic or too restrictive for dealing with the wide-ranging theological challenge that the positive approach to plurality promises. However, my observations during the intervening years are that the criticisms are usually based on a misapprehension which fails to realize that each type of response is capable of embracing a number of different forms. I defended the typology in 1993, and continue to find it useful in so far as the positions it describes are well represented in the ever-expanding literature.[2] Paul Knitter has generously defended the typology, even at the expense of some of his own carefully crafted suggestions, thus: 'these three classifications represent in broad lines the differing presuppositions and approaches within recent Christian efforts to make sense of the many religions.'[3] Knitter adds the caveat that theological models are only illuminating so long as they are treated as a 'workable framework' and leave room for expansion and modification. This is a comment with which I am happy to concur and I accept that it applies also in the search for a Christian theology of religions.

I shall now describe briefly and offer some comments on each type of approach, and give reasons why I consider the pluralist case as the one which does best justice to all of the factors involved. Towards the end of my discussion I shall return to the issue of the typology's usefulness in order to note how the critic's dismissal of it is often a rhetorical device for reinstating more conservative proposals.

Exclusivism

Exclusivism is the view that only in Christian faith can the authentic truth of God's offer of 'transcendent vision and human transformation' in the world be found. Let the following citation serve as an example of this position:

> The Gospel of Jesus Christ comes to us with a built-in prejudgment of all other faiths so that we know in advance of our study what we must ultimately conclude about them. They give meanings to life apart from that which God has given in the biblical story culminating with Jesus Christ, and they organize life outside the covenant community of Jesus Christ. Therefore, devoid of this saving knowledge and power of God, they actually lead men away from God and hold them captive before God. This definitive and blanket judgment . . . is not derived from our investigation of the religions but is given in the structure and content of Gospel faith itself.[4]

This argument is forcefully made. It accepts that what is at stake is not a comparison of religious benefits, fruits or experiences but a theological judgement. It is simply that those who 'organize life outside the covenant community of Jesus Christ' are not recipients of divine grace. 'Christian faith' and 'the rest' are different species. But more is involved, especially when the writer avers that other traditions 'actually lead men away from God'. How does the writer know this? The answer is that it is dogmatically 'given in the structure and content of Gospel faith itself'.

I suggest that in fact there are two main principles at work in this citation. First, there is an appeal to the theological notion of revelation – 'God has given'; and second, there is the confessional clinging to the 'structure and content of Gospel faith itself'. Let me respond to both these aspects of Exclusivism.

First, no matter how varied the form or emphasis of a particular theory of revelation, we need to remember that the awareness of revelation is essentially a voluntary act.[5] Thus, according to one philosopher of religion: 'authentic religion is the gratuitous human response to a gratuitous revelation of the divine'.[6] In other words, the human response to revelation cannot simply be one of passive reception in the face of given divine revelation. In the voluntary act of its recognition, revelation is both experienced as gift and creatively appropriated, moulded and interpreted via the human religious imagination.

At the heart of Exclusivism is the incipient claim to have received a kind of 'neat' revelation; and it is this which creates the impression of its arbitrariness. But the gratuitousness of revelation cannot be circumnavigated. It is a means for rejoicing in what has been discovered, received and shaped, but from it there is no plausible argument that leads inexorably to the condemnation of other faith-traditions. One could push the point further: the awareness of this gratuitousness, coupled with the insight about the universality of the divine presence to which the gift of faith is a response, alerts us to the expectation that the experience and knowledge of Ultimate Reality may not be confined to one instance of its particular apprehension.

The second cause for concern with Exclusivism is the appeal to the 'structure and content of Gospel faith itself' with its background in the 'biblical story' as a whole. Setting aside the very real difficulties with the basic exegetical-theological conception of a single 'biblical story culminating with Jesus Christ', how are we to interpret the biblical literature in respect of 'other religions'? The Bible is often assumed to be 'against' other religions. But this is obviously too simple a judgement. There are numerous examples of divine involvement with different peoples. God may have 'chosen' his people Israel, but he also calls 'others': 'Did I not bring up Israel from the land of Egypt, and the Philistines from Caphtor and the Syrians from Kir?,' declares the eighth-century (BCE) prophet Amos (9.7). And in the Christian New Testament, the evangelist Matthew, for example, accepts that those who do the will of the Father are welcomed into the kingdom of heaven and not just those who call out the Lord's name (Matt. 25.31–46). Moving beyond literalism, the question is how to interpret the Bible's 'particularity' (or set of particularities) in relation to its 'universal' impulses. This is both an exegetical question in relation to historically conditioned material, and a hermeneutical question arising from the need for theological translation in a vastly different historical context.

A more broadly based analysis of the 'biblical story' has been suggested by the Catholic scholars, Donald Senior and Carroll Stuhlmueller. Following an in-depth survey of the biblical literature in relation to mission, they accept that 'a staggering question for the contemporary church is that of Christianity's relationship to non-Christian religions'. They then draw the startling exegetical conclusion: 'No comprehensive solution to this issue can be found in the Bible.' Perhaps that is hardly surprising, for the biblical writers were not faced precisely by our contemporary realities. In terms of the hermeneutical possibilities, however, Senior and Stuhlmueller continue, '[the Bible] does offer some leads'.[7] The leads they suggest build on the universal intuitions of biblical history. These accept that the activity of God extends beyond the immediate experiences of Israel and the first churches in complex and dialectical ways – in the validity of the religious experiences of other peoples/cultures and through the pervasive divine presence in creation and world history. The final conclusion of Senior and Stuhlmueller is that 'the God of the Bible sends his people out to reveal and to discover his love in places beyond sectarian borders'.

The advantage of this broad-based approach to the 'biblical story' is that it does draw the sting of those whose stand on the authority of scripture assumes that it leads to an exclusivist-type approach in the theology of religions. The discovery of God 'beyond sectarian borders' is a far cry from the 'definitive and blanket judgment' envisaged by the exclusivist citation above. The issue of what form a creative theology of religions might take in the changed plural conditions of today can only be answered with reference to the wider debate surrounding biblical hermeneutics.

Inclusivism

In the theological negotiation between the poles of particularity and universality, exclusivist views end up by recasting the polarity as a contradiction. The second type of Christian response in the theology of religions claims to balance the two poles by honouring two so-called theological axioms: (1) the affirmation that Christian salvation has been made effective in the world through its embodiment in the person of Jesus Christ (particularity), and (2) the belief in the universal will of God to save all peoples (universality). Let the official Catholic encyclical, *Redemptoris Missio*, sum up this point of view:

> The universality of salvation means that it is granted not only to those who explicitly believe in Christ and have entered the Church. Since salvation is offered to all, it must be made concretely available to all. But it is clear that today, as in the past, many people do not have an opportunity to come to know or accept the Gospel revelation or to enter the Church. The social and cultural conditions in which they live do not permit this, and frequently they have been brought up in other religious traditions. For such people salvation in Christ is accessible by virtue of a grace which, while having a mysterious relationship to the Church, does not make them formally part of the Church but enlightens them in a way which is accommodated to their spiritual and material situation. This grace comes from Christ; it is the result of his Sacrifice and is communicated by the Holy Spirit. It enables each person to attain salvation through his or her free co-operation.
>
> Although participated forms of mediation of different kinds and degrees are not excluded, they acquire meaning and value *only* from Christ's own mediation, and they cannot be understood as parallel or complementary to his.[8]

With the absorption of historical consciousness, inclusivism accepts that elements of religious value and truth springing from God's universal presence in creation and history are necessarily embodied in tradition. Therefore other traditions *per se* can be vehicles of Christian saving grace. Many theologians from the three main branches of the Christian tree now accept the general thrust of the inclusivist outlook.

However, I want to draw attention to three problems associated with this approach. First, in order to demonstrate how it is that the grace of Christ is experienced without knowing or naming it as such from within the historical life of other faith-traditions, some 'theological linkage' between Christian faith and other traditions needs to be specified. In the past, the notion of 'fulfilment' provided the conceptual assurance of this linkage, but this is now generally thought to be problematic (see Chapter 3). More recent theories of the inclusivist type are likely to seek some less predetermined possibility of 'spiritual association' between Christian faith and other faith-traditions. But the overall aim is to demonstrate how the Christian witness to ultimate truth makes explicit that which is at work implicitly through the witness of others.

Such an aim need not necessarily be interpreted as a triumphalistic move. Indeed, many inclusivist-minded theologians also acknowledge the rich possibilities by which other religions might even complement Christianity's sense of its own witness to religious truth. Nevertheless, the overriding impression remains that Christian faith retains the spiritual and theological edge on others. As the inclusivist Jacques Dupuis says: 'Salvation is at work everywhere; but in the concrete figure of the crucified Christ the work of salvation is seen to be accomplished.'[9] It seems to me that it is virtually impossible to establish a 'theological linkage' that is not already tailored to Christian supremacy.

The second problem with inclusivism concerns the meaning which can be attached to the notion of Christ's 'Sacrifice' extending to other religions. How can an historical event-cum-belief – the death and resurrection of Jesus – be effective retroactively before the life of Jesus himself? How can it extend to the Buddhist tradition which began 500 years prior to Christianity, or to the Hindu, Jain or Primal traditions whose origins date back further? The notion seems highly improbable.

One way round this difficulty is to point not to the *origins* of salvation in the historical Jesus but to the *climactic expression* of his universal effectiveness through the presence of the *logos* which he is said to embody and exhibit in quintessential measure. This route recalls and builds on theories of the early Christian Apologists. These were Christian philosophers who praised the light of divine reason in other religious philosophies while simultaneously affirming that the grounding and summation of that light was found in the person of Jesus. In doing so they were able to accept that those who practised justice and 'the good' received a share in the divine life, which nevertheless had eventually declared itself 'enfleshed' in the historical life of Jesus. The important point about this 'logos-Christ' doctrine is that, apart from its abstraction, Jesus 'saves' by embodying the goal of the religious life rather than by initiating a process of salvation dating from the fixed time of Jesus himself. In other words, the importance of Jesus is less his 'Sacrifice' and more his normative value (a lesser sounding judgemental measure) in comparison with other saviour or revealer figures. Nevertheless, we are back here with having to 'prove' that normative value, spiritually or historically. To date I know of no case that demonstrates such normativity beyond its formal theological supposition.

It seems that honouring the two axioms along the inclusivist way brings unmanageable problems. The contradictions felt with exclusivist views are lessened, but the pull between the two axioms remains unresolved. As Paul Knitter has put it: 'It does not seem possible to maintain this traditional insistence on the ontological necessity of Christ for salvation and at the same time coherently profess belief in the universal salvific will of the Christian God.'[10] I shall take up the christological aspects of Inclusivism in Chapter 4.

Some theologians, feeling the weight of the kind of critique I have just offered, have turned more to other Christian ideas in order to devise strategies which seek to combine universality with particularity. The theological symbols of the Spirit or the kingdom of God are said to offer an attractive alternative route for engaging with other religions, without any sense of prejudging that the direct christological approaches seem to involve. The Spirit can be viewed as the 'free agent' of God's universal presence, independent of Christ or the church; and the kingdom signifies the eschatological reality of God's final rule which runs ahead, as it were, of all religions. 'Christ' neither exhausts the Spirit's activity nor forecloses kingdom-shaped realities discovered through dialogue and collaboration.

In other words, the universal-sounding language of the kingdom and the Spirit would seem to be exempt from the historical problems inherent in christological inclusivism. 'The kingdom' summons both the church and other faith-communities to a profound commitment to a more peaceful and equitable society. So 'kingdom' values are advanced each time the poor win justice, or when one small corner of the planet is shielded from further ecological devastation. The activity too of the 'Spirit' is not bound by its Christian expression. It 'blows where it wills', inspiring a vision of the spiritual life wherever human beings catch a glimpse of ultimate meaning and transcend their ego-centred existence.

However, my own view is that these moves do not really resolve the central difficulty. The reason has been given, again, by Dupuis:

> While the believers of other religious faiths perceive God's call through their own traditions and respond to it in the sincere practice of these traditions, they become in all truth – even without being formally conscious of it – active members of the Kingdom. In the final analysis, then, a theology of religions following the Kingdom-centered model cannot bypass or avoid the Christocentric perspective.[11]

Yet, as we have seen, it is the christocentric perspective, which is so problematic for Inclusivism.

Pluralism

Just as Exclusivism and Inclusivism contain a spectrum of forms, the same is true of the third option, Pluralism. At the outset, however, we should dismiss the easy misunderstanding – even caricature – of this position. This is the proposal that the many religions worship and believe in the same God and that therefore religious differences and philosophical and theological clashes between different religions in their reflective-systematic dimensions are irrelevant. There is no serious pluralist theologian of religions, of whom I know, that advocates this view in the Christian theology of religions debate.

There is of course a related and serious position, situated within a Hindu philosophical ethos that comes close to this outlook. Consider, for example, Swami Vivekananda's image of a circle with different radii as an explanation of the unity-in-diversity of the religions:

> If it be true that God is the center of all religions, and that each of us is moving towards Him along one of these radii, then it

is certain that all of us *must* reach that center. And at the center where all radii meet, all our differences will cease; but until we reach there, differences there must be.[12]

Vivekananda was a follower of Advaita Vedanta, a non-dual form of Hinduism that distinguishes between higher (i.e. philosophical non-duality) and lower (i.e. devotional worship of deities) levels of religious apprehension and practice. What he achieved was the expansion in modern times of a particular Hindu philosophy – one that had developed in one cultural setting over many centuries in order to accommodate a variety of religious expressions and practices – to explain an even greater awareness of contemporary global religious life. Variety is to be expected; but the goal of the religions remains the same: that 'they are true manifestations of the same truth, and that they all lead to the same conclusions as the *advaita* has reached'.[13]

There is much more to the views of Vivekananda than I have depicted here. However, it is clear that to adopt Advaita Vedanta as the solution to the challenges of religious plurality would be essentially to adopt a form of Inclusivism based on a Hindu outlook. The *advaitic* notion of the divine has supplied the controlling image of Ultimate Reality and all other images are subservient to this. The Pluralism that I have in mind, on the other hand, moves beyond the controlling images of any one of the religions.

One of the foremost exponents of a philosophically tuned and religiously motivated Pluralism is John Hick, who has propounded, developed and defended his views over a number of years.[14] Let the following citation set the scene:

If salvation is taking place, and taking place to about the same extent, within the religious systems presided over by these various deities and absolutes, this suggests that they are different manifestations to humanity of a yet more ultimate ground of all salvific transformation . . .

If, then, we proceed inductively from the phenomenon of religious experience around the world, adopting a religious as distinguished from a naturalistic interpretation of it, we are likely to find ourselves making two moves. The first is to postulate an ultimate transcendent divine reality (which I have been referring to as the Real) which, being beyond the scope of our human concepts, cannot be directly experienced by us as it is in itself but only as it appears through our various human thought-forms. And the second is to identify the thought-and-experienced deities and absolutes as different manifestations of the Real within different historical forms of human consciousness.[15]

Pluralists accept that the religions, when conceived merely as systems of belief, are bound to exhibit conflicting beliefs at conceptual levels. However, as contexts of 'transcendent vision and human transformation' the religions are not primarily systems of philosophical and theological rationality, although of course they do involve themselves in extensive reflective processes and are shaped in large measure by them. But if the issue of plurality is approached from the perspective of the *transformative* purpose for which the religions exist, then a different possibility in the theology of religions becomes available.

Let me now set out the pluralist approach in a number of steps:

1 The authenticity and truth of the Christian Way is based on the validity of the religious experience it embodies; i.e. the basic Christian affirmation of 'transcendent vision and human transformation' is trustworthy as real experience and it has cognitive implications.

2 This Christian act of trustworthiness can be extended to others on the basis that other religious contexts too provide a framework for 'transcendent vision and human transformation'; i.e. there is no reason to doubt the validity of the religious apprehension of other religious traditions and every reason to accept their integrity.

3 The spiritual fruits of the many faith-traditions seem comparable: all have inspired saints and holy figures who have been active on either individual or sociopolitical levels (or both), and all have demonstrated their share of complicity in support of different kinds of social ills, such as racism,

war, sexual prejudice, and so on; i.e. the comparability of spiritual fruits suggests a common source of inspiration, however this is portrayed in different traditions.

4 The distinction occurring in all faith-traditions between the 'unknowability' and the 'knowability' of Ultimate Reality in terms of symbolic/iconic forms is the key distinction which allows for the hypothesis of Ultimate Reality to be experienced and conceptualized in different symbolic/iconic forms according to cultural history; i.e. Ultimate Reality as ineffable is yet the deeper ground of the varied manifestations of ultimacy glimpsed through the varied lenses of the historical and cultural forms of the religions themselves.

5 Theologies and religious philosophies have evolved within particular cultural environments, reflecting the limitations of these environments, but the faith-traditions now need to develop new directions for their theologies and philosophies in order to account for the wider picture encompassed by religious plurality. In Christianity, this entails formulating Christian belief in a manner which respects the integrity of other traditions; i.e. the effectiveness of Christian belief need not depend on theological interpretations which are treated as necessarily absolute and/or exclusive.

6 Criteria for distinguishing between good and bad religion, and between true and false religion need to be developed; i.e. in order to dispel the relativist caricature that 'anything goes' pluralists have an ongoing task to specify critically the grounds on which certain manifestations of religion are more and less acceptable.

7 Each tradition has both an adequate and inadequate grasp of the relationship between particularity and universality; i.e. each particular vision of the universal availability of Ultimate Reality is an adequate (if also conditioned and partial) view of the whole yet complementary to other equally adequate (if also conditioned and partial) perspectives of the whole.

8 Belief systems are practical means for achieving the religious ends of 'transcendent vision and human transformation'. While this entails that many metaphysical and other disagreements between traditions will remain it does not invalidate the basic picture of complementarity; i.e. patterns of what

constitutes complementarity can be pursued through critical dialogue, in mutual respect and without prejudice.

Although this list of points building up the pluralist option is rather telescoped down, I trust it provides an accurate statement of at least one main form of the pluralist option.[16] It marks a break with exclusivist and inclusivist outlooks because it does not interpret religious plurality from the perspective of Christian absolutism. It allows for the distinctiveness of the Christian voice, but it neither elevates Christian faith into a position of superiority, finality, unsurpassability, or exclusivity, nor renders other faith-traditions as lesser versions of what has emerged through the greater Christian tradition.

In terms of the tension between the particularity and universality of Ultimate Reality in its Christian form, Pluralism recognizes that the affirmation of universality is not the evocation of a generalized sense of divine presence in creation and history but turns out to be an affirmation of a series of differently centred and organized religious particularities, each with their own validity.

Some Objections

A number of overlapping criticisms of the pluralist option have been expressed from different perspectives. Let me respond now, in a preliminary way, to criticisms raised roughly from the three perspectives of Religious Studies, Philosophy and Theology. I shall reserve a fuller discussion of the issues for Chapter 6.

First, specialists from a Religious Studies background might complain that the tendency of Pluralism is towards assuming similarities where in fact great divergences exist. My phrase 'transcendent vision and human transformation', it could be argued, pre-empts what we are to think of the religions prior to their actual encounter. The religions display different views of what is 'transcendent' and different recommendations for 'human transformation'. While it is true that the religions are radically particular when viewed as whole apprehensions of religious life, I do not myself think that this necessarily undermines the point, outlined in Chapter 1, that a generic Cycle of

Religious Life is a legitimate inference to make based on observation and experience. The alternative picture is that we accept that each religion is locked into its own version of what constitutes the meaning of life. But this seems hardly attractive, let alone possible in today's global interconnectedness. Citing Max Müller's famous line – 'he who knows one religion . . . knows none' – the American scholar of religions, Rita Gross, follows this with the observation: 'One cannot understand the specificity and uniqueness of one's religion if one does not have a basis for comparison.'[17] This far-reaching remark undercuts the drive towards isolationism. From a pluralist perspective it provides backing for the intention in the hypothesis to honour both the radical differences between the religions and their transcendent origins in the ineffability of Ultimate Reality.

Second, a common objection from a philosophical angle against Pluralism is that it is dependent on European Enlightenment patterns of rationality precisely at a time when these patterns are coming under severe criticism. The Enlightenment, it is claimed, sought to achieve a 'totalizing' universal rationality based on secular premises, and it is this claim to 'totalizing' universality which is now being questioned. This criticism, it seems to me, is misplaced. For there is a distinction surely between the inflated claims of a (secular) philosophical theory, which allegedly provides the world with the so-called final 'grand narrative', and the now fairly generally accepted observation that conditions of history and culture have played a large part in shaping the thought-forms, frameworks of interpretation, and conceptual apparatus attaching to faith-traditions. One can take advantageous note of the latter while disowning the former.

Accepting the human conditions attaching to religious beliefs, traditions, symbolic patterns, and so on, does not mean that Pluralism is a form of secularism. Again, as Rita Gross has shown:

> Upon further reflection, it becomes clear that acknowledging the human component and the cultural relativity of religion in no way threatens the validity or relevance of religion in general or of any specific religion. Beneath all the culturally

relative and culture-bound symbols or beliefs, and at the heart of the human creativity and responsiveness generating religious symbols and beliefs, is That Which stimulates such responses.[18]

In other words, Pluralism does not erect another grand narrative, so much as follow through the consequences of philosophical observations about how knowledge comes to human consciousness and then applies this in the realm of (plural) religious consciousness. So the differences between the names given to 'That Which' is conceived of as ultimate in the different religious traditions are differences between different phenomenal manifestations of the one noumenal Ultimate Reality. They are not differences between different names for the same directly accessible ultimate referent.

Turning now, third, to the theological area of objection, a number of theologians complain that Pluralism can never be fully embraced as a Christian option because it is based on premises other than those ruled by the governing Christian idea of Christ. For example, Christoph Schwöbel has written: 'From the perspective of Christian faith there is no escape from the universality of God's presence in the particularity of religions. The particular constitution of this conviction, however, excludes the theological possibility of talking about a plurality of revelations in the religions.'[19] Schwöbel insists that we only know about the universal presence of Ultimate Reality by virtue of Christ. Of course, if revelation is defined as a Christian term then there will obviously be no revelation outside the Christian appreciation of it! But it is exactly this confinement of terms which the experience of plurality calls into question. Christian revelation speaks of the revelation of the love of God in Christ. Are we to think that nothing of love could be discovered outside the Christian revealing of it? Schwöbel would not wish to confine the reality of love to Christian practice only; far from it. But the belief that it is permissible for a Christian to recognize the love that is bound to exist elsewhere only in terms of its Christian definition seems to me to be frankly odd. The scriptures, theologies and practices of other religious-traditions are full of references to love.[20]

Reaffirming the Typology

For the remainder of this chapter, I would like to return to the question of the viability of the threefold typology: Exclusivism, Inclusivism and Pluralism. As I noted earlier, there have been numerous calls to abandon the typology on the grounds that it fails to take accurate account of the views of a number of serious theologians. So Wesley Ariarajah, for example, claims: 'The debate on the theology of religions needs to be much more nuanced than these positions would allow.'[21] However, I am inclined to think that the typology is roughly a correct guide because a number of writers who express a desire to move beyond it, when they submit their own positive proposals, turn out to exemplify one of the three positions. Most often this turns out to be the inclusivist one. An instructive example of this can be found in the Church of England's Doctrine Commission Report, entitled *The Mystery of Salvation* (1995). The report advocates 'moving beyond any one of these three positions', only to reinstate a view based directly on the two axioms of Inclusivism:

(1) We do assert that God can and does work in people of other religions, and indeed within other religions, and that this is by his Spirit.

(2) In the ultimate sense, salvation is defined by having Jesus Christ as its source and goal.[22]

The report finally calls for an eschatological resolution of the issue of 'salvation' whereby Christ will be acknowledged as 'the definitive focus of salvation in its fully comprehensive meaning'.[23]

Perhaps we should be grateful to the Doctrine Commission for clarifying the extent to which the typology remains valid, even as it is disowned! However, what was misleading was for the report to insist that the typology has been superseded and then offer a variation (albeit generously sculptured) of the inclusivist approach. Other examples in the Christian theology of religions, which are often based on the doctrine of the Trinity pursue a similar strategy.[24] I shall discuss some of these in Chapters 6 and 8.

It is true that some serious positions in the Christian theology of religions appear not to fall neatly within the classification. Before concluding this chapter, therefore, let me comment on two examples that come under this rubric. The first appears to be situated on the borders between Exclusivism and Inclusivism, and the second seems to fall between Inclusivism and Pluralism.

First, those who affirm the universal activity of God outside the church in individuals, but believe that there is no warrant for supporting the claim that other faith-traditions as such can be viewed as 'vehicles of salvation', are moving beyond the strict end of Exclusivism and are edging towards Inclusivism. The missiologist, Lesslie Newbigin, typified this position, and it has been claimed that the views of the later Karl Barth, which allowed for 'secular parables of the kingdom' outside Christian faith, can be extended in principle to provide grounds for inter-religious dialogue from a Christian perspective.[25] But from my point of view, in so far as a theory retains the absoluteness of the Christian message (as did Barth and Newbigin) and refrains from considering the possibility that other faith-traditions as 'hidden', 'implicit' or 'anonymous' vehicles of saving grace, then it bears the essential marks of Exclusivism.

Furthermore, there is a good reason why Exclusivism and Inclusivism are not always capable of being distinguished succinctly from one another. In so far as exclusivist thinking has a universalist aspect (recognizing the general divine presence throughout creation) and therefore leans towards inclusivist thinking, and in so far as inclusivist thinking bases its universal emphasis (recognizing other faith-traditions as vehicles of 'salvation') on Christian absolutism and therefore leans towards exclusivist thinking, Exclusivism and Inclusivism are two sides of the same coin. They are distinguished mainly by their attitudes towards other faith-traditions as valid vehicles of what I have called 'transcendent vision and human transformation'.

The real dividing-line is between those who wish to retain Christian absoluteness and those who are willing to surrender it. And this brings me to the second area of ambiguity where Inclusivism and Pluralism appear to overlap. An example of this ambiguity can be found in a helpful series of propositions listed by the Australian philosopher of religion, Max Charlesworth. Setting his views out as a *credo*, Charlesworth writes:

1 I believe that 'God' wills that all should be saved or achieve enlightenment and that all human beings have access to the means of salvation or enlightenment through some mode of revelation.

2 I believe (as a Christian, or a Jew, or a Muslim, or a Hindu or Buddhist etc.) that my religious tradition has a privileged and paradigmatic status and that 'God' has revealed himself more completely in that tradition.

3 I believe that certain authentic religious values which are implicit or latent within my tradition, but which have not actually been developed within that tradition, may be manifested or expressed in other religious traditions.

4 I believe that there is also the possibility of authentic religious revelations, complementary to the paradigmatic revelation of my tradition but 'outside' my own tradition.

5 I believe that 'God's revelation' will only be known in its fullness when, as an ideal limit, all the 'revelations' and their 'developments' are brought together in some way.

6 I believe that religious diversity is in some sense willed by 'God' and has its own intrinsic meaning and purpose and is not merely the result of sin and ignorance.

7 I believe that respect for, openness to, and dialogue with, other religious traditions, must be part of any authentic religious tradition.[26]

This position looks to be pluralist-minded but in fact it embraces a form of Inclusivism that many may well find generous and attractive. It allows for the integrity of different traditions, seeks complementarity in a greater fullness, yet pulls back from Pluralism by advocating the 'privileged and paradigmatic status' of one tradition. Part of the reason for this, Charlesworth explains, is that pluralist theories rely on philosophical frameworks of a Neoplatonic kind – where the one Ultimate divine Reality is experienced and expressed in numerous concrete historical forms – and the problem is that some traditions, such as Buddhism or Confucianism, simply do not recognize this type of philosophical framework. For example, Buddhist 'emptiness', it has been said, is equated with ultimate truth itself and is not to be transcended in some higher notion.[27]

Charlesworth's objection can be met by invoking the notion of ineffability, which all traditions acknowledge in their varying respects. Christian theology has always accepted that any image of God does not exhaust the reality of God and to that extent images of God are pointers to, or culturally conditioned interpretations of the ineffable character of God's ultimacy. Similarly, the Buddhist notion of 'emptiness' is best interpreted as the radical negation of all forms of religious apprehension which seek to offer a definitive characterization of Ultimate Reality that is uncharacterizable because it is ineffable. Edward Conze, the celebrated authority on Buddhism, has written about the analogous relationship between different views of Ultimate Reality: 'The Buddhist idea of ultimate reality is very much akin to the philosophical notion of the 'Absolute', and not easily distinguished from the notion of God among the more mystical theologians, like Dionysius Areopagita and Eckhart.'[28] And one merit of Hick's well-known distinction between 'the Real *an sich*' (ultimate transcategorial reality) and the 'personae' (the 'Gods' of theistic traditions) together with the 'impersonae' (the 'non-personal absolutes' of non-theistic traditions) – with the latter acting as manifestations of the former to human consciousness in different religious faith-traditions – is that it was developed in order to encompass both theistic and non-theistic religious experiences within an overarching hypothesis.[29] It does not equate the theistic images of God with Buddhist notions of Emptiness (or with advaita Hindu notions of Ultimate Reality as Brahman), and so on, but accepts their analogous comparability.

Without these distinctions the contradiction in Charlesworth's theses, namely, the retention of a 'privileged status' for one tradition while embracing positively the revelatory power of other faith-traditions, cannot be resolved. This is what renders his views inclusivist at the end of the day. Otherwise, his *credo* clarifies the elements of a pluralist understanding well.

This chapter has examined a spectrum of debate in the Christian theology of religions or Track One of interfaith encounter.

It advocates Pluralism as a reasonable hypothesis to explain the persistence of the many faith-traditions in relationship to Christian faith. More exactly, I have outlined only one form of Pluralism, but I am aware that pluralist approaches are not of a single kind. In particular, I have not engaged with the imaginative and substantial writings of the Christian theologian, Paul Knitter, whose evolving understanding has focused more on the theme of 'liberation' as the controlling factor in the pluralist outlook, rather than on the more philosophical aspects of the hypothesis considered here.[30] Also, in line with the scheme of the book, I have not as yet directly engaged with the Christian theology of religions debate in the light of the mushrooming dialogue between the faith-traditions. Perspectives and questions from that quarter that have a bearing on the theology of religions will be addressed in later chapters, and particularly in Chapter 6.

Notes

1 Stanley Samartha, *One Christ – Many Religions*, Maryknoll: Orbis Press 1991, p. 79.

2 See my *Christians and Religious Pluralism: Patterns in the Christian Theology of Religions*, London: SCM Press and Maryknoll: Orbis Press 1983. A second edition, published by SCM Press in 1993, embodied some minor corrections and was expanded to include a final chapter, 'Ten Years Later: Surveying the Scene', which defended the typology.

3 Paul Knitter, *One Earth, Many Religions: Multifaith Dialogue and Global Responsibility*, Maryknoll: Orbis Press 1995, p. 26.

4 Edmund Perry, *The Gospel in Dispute: The Relation of Christian Faith to Other Missionary Religions*, Doubleday: New York 1958, pp. 18f., and cited by Wilfred Cantwell Smith, 'The Christian in a Religiously Plural World', *Christianity and Other Religions: Selected Readings*, ed. John Hick and Brian Hebblethwaite, Glasgow: Collins, Fount Paperbacks 1980, p. 140.

5 See, for example, Avery Dulles, *Models of Revelation*, Maryknoll: Orbis Books 1992.

6 Max Charlesworth, *Religious Inventions: Four Essays*, Cambridge University Press 1997, p. 10.

7 Donald Senior CP and Carroll Stuhlmueller CP, *The Biblical Foundations for Mission*, London: SCM Press 1983, p. 345.

8 Pope John Paul II, Papal Encyclical, *Redemptoris Missio*, Vatican Polyglot Press, Vatican City State 1990.

9 Jacques Dupuis SJ, *Toward a Christian Theology of Religious Pluralism*, Maryknoll: Orbis Press 1997, p. 328.

10 Paul Knitter, *No Other Name? A Critical Survey of Christian Attitudes Toward the World Religions*, London: SCM Press 1985, p. 116. Maurice Wiles' analysis of the tension in Karl Rahner between the emphasis on the universal self-gift of God to the world and the unsurpassability of Jesus Christ for salvation makes the same point. It is also endorsed by Roger Haight SJ, *Jesus: Symbol of God*, Maryknoll: Orbis Books 1999, p. 422.

11 Dupuis, *Toward a Christian Theology of Religious Pluralism*, p. 345.

12 *The Complete Works of Swami Vivekananda*, Mayavati Memorial Edition, Calcutta: Advaita Ashrama, 8 vols 1964–71, vol. 2, pp. 384f., and cited by Anantanand Rambachan, 'Swami Vivekananda: A Hindu Model for Interreligious Dialogue', *Inter-Religious Dialogue: Voices from a New Frontier*, ed. M. Darrol Bryant and Frank Flinn, New York: Paragon House 1989, p. 18.

13 Rambachan, 'Swami Vivekananda', p. 11. Also note Ninian Smart's observation in *The World's Religions: Old Traditions and Modern Transformations*, Cambridge: Cambridge University Press 1989, p. 395, that 'Vivekananda's Neo-Vedanta also made sense of Hinduism for perhaps the first time. Now Hindus could explain the unity of their own baffling, diverse religion or religions.'

14 See his magisterial treatment of Pluralism in, John Hick, *An Interpretation of Religion: Human Responses to the Transcendent*, Basingstoke: Macmillan 1989; a shorter statement and creative defence of Pluralism against critics can be found in *The Rainbow of Faiths: Critical Dialogues on Religious Pluralism*, London: SCM Press 1995, and published as *A Christian Theology of Religions*, Louisville KY: Westminster/John Knox 1995; in the context of christology, see *The Metaphor of God Incarnate*, London: SCM Press 1993.

15 John Hick, 'Religious Pluralism and Salvation', *Faith and Philosophy*, vol. 5, no. 4, October 1988, p. 370; reprinted in *The Metaphor of God Incarnate*, p. 140.

16 See John Hick and Paul F. Knitter (eds), *The Myth of Christian Uniqueness: Toward a Pluralistic Theology of Religions*, London: SCM Press and Maryknoll: Orbis Press 1987, for a range of forms of Pluralism.

17 Rita Gross, 'Religious Pluralism: Some Implications for Judaism', *Journal of Ecumenical Studies* XXVI, no.1, Winter 1989, p. 41.

18 Gross, 'Religious Pluralism', p. 39.

19 Christoph Schwöbel, 'Particularity, Universality, and the Religions', *Christian Uniqueness Reconsidered: the Myth of a Pluralistic Theology of Religions*, ed. Gavin D'Costa, Maryknoll: Orbis Books 1990, p. 39.

20 Cf. John Hick's reply to Gavin D'Costa on the same point:

'Straightening the Record: Some Responses to Critics', *Modern Theology* 6, no. 2, January 1990.

21 S. Wesley Ariarajah, 'The Need for a New Debate', *The Uniqueness of Jesus: A Dialogue with Paul F. Knitter*, ed. Leonard Swidler and Paul Mojzes, Maryknoll: Orbis Press 1997, p. 30.

22 The Doctrine Commission of the Church of England, *The Mystery of Salvation*, London: Church House Publishing 1995, pp. 171, 181, 184.

23 *The Mystery of Salvation*, p. 184.

24 E.g. Gavin D'Costa, *The Meeting of Religions and the Trinity*, Edinburgh: T&T Clark, and Maryknoll: Orbis Press 2000; J. A. DiNoia OP, *The Diversity of Religions: A Christian Perspective*, Washington: Catholic University of America Press, 1992.

25 Lesslie Newbigin, *The Gospel in a Pluralist Society*, London: SPCK 1989, chapter 14; and David Lochead, *The Dialogical Imperative*, London: SCM Press 1989 and Maryknoll: Orbis Press 1988, chapter 6. From a Catholic perspective and for different reasons, Gavin D'Costa in his book, *The Meeting of Religions and the Trinity*, Edinburgh: T&T Clark and Maryknoll: Orbis Press 2000 has, in my judgement, moved near to this position. I discuss D'Costa's response to Pluralism in Chapter 6.

26 Max Charlesworth, *Religious Inventions: Four Essays*, Cambridge University Press 1997, p. 50. The author acknowledges the linguistic difficulty in denoting Ultimate Reality, and he takes it to indicate any source of disclosure or revelation.

27 Charlesworth cites Paul Williams, 'Some Dimensions of the Recent Work of Raimundo Panikkar: A Buddhist Perspective', *Religious Studies* 27, 1991, p. 520.

28 Edward Conze, *Buddhism: Its Essence and Development*, New York: Harper Torchbooks 1975, p. 111.

29 See the article 'Ineffability' by John Hick, *Religious Studies* 36, 2000, pp. 35–46, for a discussion of the concept in the context of religious plurality and in the light of philosophical criticism. See also, 'The Real and Its Personae and Impersonae', *Disputed Questions in Theology and the Philosophy of Religion*, Basingstoke: Macmillan Press 1993, chapter 10, for a well-considered response to the form of the objection to Pluralism raised by Charlesworth. In his recent writings, Hick has substituted the term 'transcategorial' for 'ineffable'.

30 See his studies *One Earth Many Religions* and *Jesus and the Other Names: Christian Mission and Global Responsibility*, Maryknoll: Orbis Press 1996. See also John Hick and Paul F. Knitter (eds), *The Myth of Christian Uniqueness*.

3

The Jewish–Christian Filter

It is no exaggeration to say that the Jewish–Christian relation-ship has played a determinative role in shaping Christian ap-proaches to other religious traditions. Indeed, so strong has this role been that it seems safe to assume that by unravelling the issues at the heart of Christian approaches to Judaism we shall clarify what is at stake in the Christian theology of religions.

But is this assumption correct? And should Jewish–Christian relations remain determinative for the future of Christian relations with people of other faiths?

On reflection, there is something curious about setting up the Christian relation to Judaism as a filter for solving the wider problem of how to interpret religious plurality. Certainly, given the fact that Christian faith has its origins in the Jewish matrix of the first century of the Common Era, Christianity feels bound to Judaism as to no other religion. This was summarized by John Paul II in his historic visit to the synagogue in Rome in 1986:

> The Jewish religion is not 'extrinsic' to us, but in a certain way is 'intrinsic' to our own religion. With Judaism, therefore, we have a relationship which we do not have with any other religion. You are our dearly beloved brothers (*sic*) and, in a certain way, it could be said that you are our elder brothers.[1]

Yet could we not also argue that it is precisely this 'intrinsic' attachment that Christianity feels towards Judaism which dis-qualifies the Jewish–Christian relationship from playing so determinative a role for the Christian response to other reli-gions in the future? How could a relationship so distinct be applicable to other relationships? The particular dynamics of

Jewish–Christian relations are different from those of, say, Buddhist–Christian or Muslim–Christian relations. And the question of an overall view of theological relationships in the Christian theology of religions is a different issue again.

There is no overriding reason, therefore, why the Jewish–Christian filter ought to be allowed to colour the contemporary Christian reckoning with religious plurality so deeply. That it has functioned to a significant degree this way historically is not a strong enough reason for allowing its causal effects a continuing role for the future. Indeed, I shall argue that there are good reasons for reversing the usual assessment, and claiming that the hiatus in the Jewish–Christian relationship is more reasonably tackled by locating it within the framework of the wider search for a Christian theology of religions.

However, in order to demonstrate why it is becoming possible to reassess the role of the Jewish–Christian filter in relation to the wider debate it is necessary to investigate more closely both its negative and positive effects. Negatively, it seems that the historic theological antagonism between Judaism and Christianity has been projected on to Christian relationships with other traditions. It is small wonder, therefore, that a similar antagonistic fate awaited Christian relations with other faith-traditions. On the other hand, the positive prospect claims that if the hiatus in Jewish–Christian relations can be overcome by the sounder application of historical, biblical and theological critical principles, the door may be opened for a positive appreciation of the wider religious plurality. Once opened, however, the particular issues of Jewish–Christian relations can take their place as part of a wider view of the relationship between religions in the Christian theology of religions.

This chapter explores three areas of theological antagonism between Jews and Christians – the theme of Christian 'fulfilment', whereby Jewish patterns of historical expectation and hope are said to come to fruition in Christian beliefs and practices; responses to the Shoah (Holocaust) in the light of the history of Christian anti-Judaism; and the interpretation of Christian scripture in relation to supercessionism, the doctrine which assumes that Christian faith supercedes Judaism. A final section will point briefly to some newly emerging dialogical patterns of

Jewish–Christian relations, patterns which I believe are more compatible with pluralist forms of thinking.

Fulfilment Theology

The 'fulfilment' linkage within the Jewish–Christian filter is not difficult to depict. From the dogmatic tradition, C. Saldanha sums it up: 'If it was the Incarnate Word crucified who *set Christianity apart* in its novelty and transcendence, it was the same Incarnate Word crucified who *brought the religions and Christianity together* in a preparation-fulfilment relationship'.[2] For Saldanha, following in the steps of the Church Fathers, claims for the Christian fulfilment of biblical prophetic hopes broadened out in church tradition into fulfilment in many dimensions. As God was at work through his *logos* or spirit in the Jewish prophets and scriptures, so he was at work in the discourses of honoured philosophers by the same *logos* or spirit.

Although many theologians in recent decades, and particularly since Vatican II, claim to have disowned fulfilment theory, its strong influence remains, as the Catholic writer, Claude Geffré has written:

> Personally, I fail to see how we can leave completely behind a certain inclusivism, that is, a theology of the *fulfillment* (to use a term present in Catholic theology since Vatican II) in Jesus Christ of all seeds of truth, goodness, and holiness contained in the religious experience of humankind.[3]

Clearly there are limits to the abolition of fulfilment theology! Geffré, however, guards against negative interpretations of fulfilment theory. His own aim, he says, is 'to reinterpret this notion of fulfillment in a non-possessive and non-totalitarian sense'. This leads him to reaffirm the absoluteness of Christ, but now 'as eschatological fullness that will never be revealed in history'.[4] Geffré expects other faith-traditions to last until the *eschaton*, when members of other faith-traditions will receive their final confrontation with Christ.

It is clear that both exclusivist and inclusivist theologies are, at root, dependent on fulfilment thinking. Referring again to the report of the Doctrine Commission of the Church of England, *The Mystery of Salvation*, (see above, p. 36) as an example of Inclusivism, this report disowns the language of fulfilment but nevertheless draws a conclusion along similar lines to that of Geffré. After affirming the belief that 'God can and does work in people of other religions, and indeed within other religions, and that this is by his Spirit', the report adds: 'We would also sensitively and firmly assert that fullness of relationship with God is possible only in Jesus Christ, who is the definitive revelation of God. For many this may happen only in an eschatological dimension (cf. 1 Cor. 15.22–28).'[5] The language of 'fullness' comes straight out of the literature of fulfilment theology. Moreover, deferring this fulfilment to 'an eschatological dimension' does nothing to ameliorate the patronizing signal that it sends to people of other faith-traditions. It is a strategy that is being emphasized in recent writing in the Christian theology of religions.[6]

In the context of the debate about the Christian–Jewish filter *vis-à-vis* other religions, perhaps it is no accident that it is Jewish writers who are often most alert to the legacy of fulfilment thinking. For example, the orthodox rabbi, David Hartman, had protested some twenty years earlier: 'We cannot in some way leap to some eschaton and live in two dimensions; to be pluralistic now but to be monistic in our eschatological vision is bad faith.'[7] Clearly, the Doctrine Commission had not read Rabbi Hartman! It seems disingenuous to discard the language of fulfilment only in order to reinstate it with an eschatological delay tag attached.

If 'fulfilment' has largely disappeared from Christian literature as a serious contender (except in biblical-literalist circles) for describing the evolving Jewish–Christian relationship, surely there is no reason why it should continue to apply in the wider theology of religions debate. Those who remain uncertain about exclusivist and inclusivist theologies of religion are, I believe, intuiting correctly the hidden dangers of fulfilment language and schemas.

My argument may be moving too quickly for some. The notion of fulfilment is deeply embedded in the Christian outlook, deriving essentially from its New Testament origins.

Does not Geffré's point, that such language can scarcely be cast aside without losing something of the central momentum of Christianity, require more serious consideration than I have so far given it? I believe that the anxiety over discarding the language of fulfilment is misplaced. At worst, such language sounds impossibly dogmatic in a plural age, and at best, it has become ambivalent. The reasons for this will I hope become clearer with the next two sections.

Shoah/Holocaust Theology

Probably more than any other influence, it has been the impact of the Shoah and 'holocaust theology' that has led Christian theologians to reassess radically their approaches to Judaism. While it is true to say that Christian anti-Judaism was not the direct cause of the Shoah, there is common consent that it formed part of the complex historical and cultural reasons that led to the Jews being viewed as a pariah people and therefore as dispensable.[8] The connection between historic Christian doctrine regarding the Jews and the practice of anti-Semitism throughout Christian history was aptly summed up by Jules Isaac in the title of his book *The Teaching of Contempt*.[9]

The rise and subsequent vehemence of the anti-Jewish (*Adversus Iudaeos*) tradition in the Church Fathers may be in part due to the threat that the continuing vibrancy of the synagogue presented to the church. But the lines of theological denigration were already becoming firmly established. Thus John Chrysostom in the fourth century, echoing his own version of Christian antipathy towards the Jews, declares: 'Indeed, not only the synagogue, but the soul of Jews are also the dwelling places of demons.'[10] It was Augustine who formalized the reprobate status of the Jews, arguing that their continued existence was necessary (and that therefore they were to be protected) as proof both of the ancient roots of Christianity and of the divine punishment that is consequent on the rejection of the Son of God.[11]

After the Shoah, the reassessment of the Christian 'teaching of contempt' has taken a number of forms. At one end of a spectrum, there have been those who have viewed anti-Semitism as an aberration in real Christian terms, an ethical failure on a massive scale and therefore requiring Christian repentance; but it was not a serious failure at a theological level. At the other end of the spectrum, Rosemary Ruether's critique of Christian anti-Judaism as the 'shadow side' of the Christian affirmation of Jesus as the Messiah – what she termed the 'left hand of christology' – remains the most trenchant call for reassessment.[12] In between are views that repudiate both the doctrines of supercessionism and the replacement of an inferior Judaism by a superior Christianity, but which retain some form of the finality of Jesus as Messiah. On the whole, the churches have more or less officially adopted this midway position. Their intentions have been to reinstate Judaism as a continuing valid covenant in God's purposes, but it remains a moot point whether the far-reaching theological consequences of repudiating supercession-ism have been fully absorbed. It is worth commenting briefly on these three types of responses a little further, in order to grasp the conclusions which can be drawn from them for developments in the Christian theology of religions.

With the first position, the Christian conscience could be salvaged if it could be shown that the theological denigration of the Jewish people resulted essentially from political developments after the conversion of Constantine and the subsequent emergence of Christendom as a religio-political empire. Better honing of historical and interpretative skills in relation to the New Testament literature would further enable us, it is claimed, to judge most of the undoubted anti-Jewish sentiment that is found in its pages as peripheral to the Christian cause. This, in turn, would leave the central Christian message unscathed. In other words, the problem has been the abuse of the Christian message, not the Christian message itself.

Yet the question remains whether the historical demonizing of the Jews can be separated so readily from Christian belief. Partly this is a matter of tracing historical influences on the Christian approaches to Judaism; partly it is a matter of drawing the distinction between Christian anti-Judaism and racial anti-Semitism. With this distinction, some claim that, although there is a link between anti-Judaism and anti-Semitism via the reality of Christendom, it is by no means obvious that the one leads directly to the other. For example, the Catholic document, 'We Remember: A Reflection on the *Shoah*', published in 1998 by the Commission for Religious Relations with the Jews, was clear where responsibility lay: 'The *Shoah* was the work of a thoroughly modern neopagan regime. Its antisemitism had its roots outside of Christianity.'[13] On this view, it should be possible to repent of Christian involvement with anti-Semitism – in so far as Christians and the churches have been caught up in its demonic clutches – without admitting that it is an inevitable consequence of anti-Judaism. In other words, no doctrinal adjustment in relation to the Jews is required as a result of the Shoah.

But it is unlikely that the distinction between anti-Judaism and anti-Semitism can be maintained in so hard and fast a manner. The denigration of the Jews began prior to the rise of Christendom, and can be traced to the roots of Christianity itself. As the Catholic scholar of Jewish–Christian relations, Gregory Baum, admits:

> What Paul and the entire Christian tradition taught is unmistakably negative: the religion of Israel is now superseded, the Torah abrogated, the promises fulfilled in the Christian Church, the Jews struck with blindness, and whatever remains of the election of Israel rests as a burden upon them in the present age.[14]

Baum may have exaggerated the extent to which this process had gone by the time the main writings of the New Testament were completed, but the overall seed of negativity is hard to ignore. It is reflected, for example, in the symbolism of John's Gospel, where the Jews are equated with 'the evil one', and who are intent on murdering Jesus (John 8.44); or, in the famous Matthean verse, 'His blood be on us and on our children' (Matt. 27.25), which has sanctioned so much violence down the centuries.

At the other end of the spectrum, among Christian theologians it has been Rosemary Ruether who has protested the most vigorously about Christian anti-Semitism. She writes:

> The anti-Semitic heritage of Christian civilization is neither an

accidental nor a peripheral element. It cannot be dismissed as
a legacy from paganism or as a product of purely sociological
conflicts between the church and the synagogue. Anti-Semitism
in Western civilization springs, at its roots, from Christian
theological anti-Judaism.[15]

Ruether's judgement is uncompromising: 'For us, who live after
the Holocaust, after the collapse of Christian eschatology into
nazi genocidal destruction, profound reassessment of this whole
heritage becomes necessary.'[16]

The essential problem, as Ruether sees it, is that the Christian
affirmation of Jesus as Messiah did not match Jewish expectations. By affirming a crucified Messiah Christians moved the
eschatalogical goalposts. On the Jewish view the expected
changes in society that would accompany the arrival of the
messianic age did not happen. In reaction to this Jewish critique
of *Christian* messianism, the Christian response was to develop
its teaching of anti-Judaism as an intrinsic part of its own credibility. In order to cut through this gordian knot, Ruether is led
to reinterpret the impact of Jesus as a proleptic anticipation of
a vision of God and the future, an anticipation in which
both Christians and Jews can share from their different
perspectives. The failure of Jesus to become the *Jewish* Messiah
falsifies neither the vision of God that stems from him, nor the
continuing validity of Judaism in Christian eyes. As Ruether
says: 'The story of Jesus parallels, it does not negate the
Exodus.'[17]

Like Baum, Ruether may have exaggerated the vehemence of
the Christian stance against Judaism so early in the church's
existence, in what must have been a very fluid period. Some have
suggested that the real problem in the early period was Christian
proselytizing and not messianic christology.[18] But to draw such
a sharp distinction between mission and christology at this early
period is unwarranted, for mission is carried out in the name of
Jesus the Messiah. On the whole, in my view Ruether's central
challenge still stands, and it is notable that many Christian
writers on Jewish–Christian relations sidestep her sharp critique.
I shall return to the issue of christology more directly in the next
chapter.

As a final comment on the spectrum of the Christian responses to anti-Judaism, let me comment briefly on the middle position that falls between slight adjustment and wholesale reappraisal. This is the mainline position of most churches. In general terms, they have denounced any continuing allegiance to describing the Jew as reprobate and owned up to some complicity in preparing the cultural ground for the Shoah. In drawing the consequences, theologically they have repudiated the doctrine of supercessionism and accepted that the covenant with the Jews remains valid. Compared to most of the Christian tradition, this amounts to a major reversal of previous attitudes. For example, the 'Consultation on the Churches and the Jewish People', held in 1988 by the World Council of Churches (WCC) at Sigtuna, Sweden, reviewed the documents issued by the WCC over a number of years of dialogue, and concluded: 'We see not one covenant displacing another, but two communities of faith, each called into existence by God, each holding its respective gifts from God, and each accountable to God.'[19] On the Catholic front, it is generally recognized that John Paul II has genuinely made more strides than any of his predecessors to reconcile Jews and Christians after the Shoah. Christians can never be separated from Judaism, for 'Whoever meets Jesus Christ meets Judaism.'[20]

The repudiation of the teaching of contempt represents a significant and historic reversal of attitude within Christian consciousness. Yet the question remains whether this welcome move has fully absorbed the theological consequences that flow from it. So the Jewish writer, David Gordis, has pointed out the ambivalence, for example, in papal pronouncements. At one level, Gordis applauds John Paul II's acceptance of the Jews 'because of the horror of the historical record and because Judaism can fit into the Christian theological structure'. But he also notes that 'significantly, the Pope never deals explicitly with Christian doctrinal anti-Judaism, or the record of Christian anti-semitism'.[21] This reluctance to deal with Christian anti-Semitism at a theological level suggests an inconsistency in the Christian response to the continuing validity of the Jewish covenant.[22]

Clearly, much has been achieved by both the churches and Christian theologians in the bid to reverse the 'teaching of contempt.' Yet its reversal has not, to date, been fully absorbed by the churches, and this too is reflected in other dialogues. If the Jewish–Christian relationship has in part shaped other bilateral relationships and the Christian theology of religions more generally, then without a reversal in this teaching regarding Judaism, the parallel equivalent of contempt in relations with other religions will similarly not be overcome.[23]

Supercessionism

In the first Christian century, the coming great gulf between the Christian church and the Jewish synagogue had not yet fully established itself. During this period, the first Christians knew themselves to be caught in the argument between loyalty to God's promises inherited from Judaism and what struck them as a new revelation through the person of Jesus. Was their faith a messianic version of Judaism or was it wholly new; or was it somewhere between? The New Testament struggle emphasizing either continuity or discontinuity of Christian faith in relation to its Jewish past reflects this anxiety.[24]

Eventually, however, the element of continuity was eclipsed, fulfilment hardened into discontinuity, and Christian supercessionism over Judaism emerged. Therefore it is necessary to unpick the arguments for supercessionism in order to clear the way for a different approach to Judaism, and a fortiori other religions, in the new globally plural era of the present. I shall endeavour to illustrate the problems with a brief glance at Paul's letter to the Romans 9–11, and at the writings of Luke-Acts, taken as a single work.

As an apostle to the gentiles, Paul is concerned to see that gentiles are accepted into the Christian community by virtue of their faith in Jesus. With their adoption 'in Christ', gentiles are not required, he argues, to follow standard Jewish practices, such as circumcision and obedience to the food laws, or even follow the Jewish law as an end in itself. This leaves many unresolved issues. What is the relationship between the gentile Christians, Jewish Christians, and the Jewish past? Paul is deeply worried by the fact that the Jewish people as a whole have not acknowledged the salvation won through Jesus. Does this entail that God's promises in history have become worthless? What of the Jewish people at the final end of the present age when Jesus returns and the new age is fully inaugurated?

It would be surprising if Paul managed to resolve all of these issues neatly for posterity, and this is not the place to explore them in detail. Suffice it to say, however, that Paul has been interpreted as stressing dominantly either discontinuity or continuity with Judaism. Singling out the famous chapters 9–11 of his letter to the Romans as the *locus classicus* of Paul's attempts to answer his own questions about his own Judaism, how successful was he?

It is often pointed out that Romans 9 stresses the discontinuity between Paul's Jewish past and his Christian present. This can be seen in Paul's explanation of his people's rejection of Jesus as being due to God hardening the people's hearts – 'God hardens whom he wills' (9.18). In a bid to protect the sovereignty of God's election promises, Paul is led, extraordinarily, to cast the Jews of his time in the shape of Pharaoh, the classical enemy of Israel. This seems like rejection with a vengeance. Salvation is through Jesus alone. On the other hand, by the time Romans 11 is complete, Paul is stressing the mystery of God's purposes, omits Christ-language, and Israel's final destiny is left in God's hands – 'God never takes back his gifts or revokes his choice' (11.29).

These ambiguities in Romans 9–11 have led to opposite interpretations: either Jesus alone is saviour or Jesus is saviour-plus-God-also-keeps-his-promises-to-the-elect-of-Israel. But the balance between these options is not equal either here or throughout Paul's writings as a whole. In times of ecumenical rapprochement, Romans 11 has been thrust to the foreground. But this may be a case of wish-fulfilment on the part of certain theologians. While the later strong contrast between Christianity and Judaism has undoubtedly in the past been read into Paul's letters (and the New Testament generally), we should also not underplay the significant difference that he thinks Jesus makes in the purposes of God. In the context of the dialogue between religions, it may be right to highlight the element of 'mystery' from Romans 11 as indicating potentially the inclusivity of Israel in God's final salvation. But as E. P. Sanders has indicated, Paul only achieves this by folding the destiny of Israel into the universal destiny of all creation.[25] There is no indication from Paul that salvation, eschatologically completed with the return of Jesus at his next coming, is to be other than in the name of Jesus.

Raising the hermeneutical question, what can be said today about Paul's struggles? I have already mentioned the biblical survey of mission by the New Testament scholars, Donald Senior and Carroll Stuhlmueller (see above, p. 24f.). In relation to the question of Christian mission and the Jews they are forthright about how open-ended the New Testament really is:

> Any solution on the part of Christians that can only see the church as the complete fulfillment of the promises to Israel and therefore considers Judaism to be an anachronistic and discarded prototype is incompatible with the Bible and with the facts of history . . .
>
> To treat Jews as one more people, as one more non-Christian religion and to embark on a strategy of individual conversion is not in the spirit of the Bible and is to be too sure of a question that the biblical people hesitated to answer.[26]

This judgement concurs with the unfinished business of Paul's thought in Romans 9–11. Paul was necessarily theologically rough-edged, in spite of what the later Christian tradition has made of him. We can accept that the issues of continuity and discontinuity remain alive today in Jewish–Christian relations, but they are not solved by reference to these three chapters alone. Precisely how they are to be addressed will depend not simply on New Testament exegesis but on a range of concerns. These include historical scholarship as well as any contribution stemming from the agenda being set by Jewish–Christian dialogue in our own day. I shall return to this point in the next section.

What now of my other chosen example of alleged supercessionist thinking, in Luke-Acts? Given Luke's theological interests and narrative style, he weaves the issue of continuity versus discontinuity into the fabric of both Jesus' ministry and the subsequent mission of his disciples in the church. Jesus is portrayed as springing from the womb of Israel (through Mary). This yields the impression that the newness which Christian faith embodies is wholly at one with the expectations of Israel's past. Jesus' enactment of the kingdom of God fulfils the prophetic promise thoroughly in his person, his deeds and activities.

In Acts the disciples then pick up where Jesus left off, for they have his 'spirit' to assist them. From the birth of Jesus at Bethlehem, via Calvary/Easter/Pentecost at Jerusalem and on to the mission of the church looking to Rome, Luke weaves a single cloth, seeking to show how the purposes of God in Jesus and the church are being fulfilled throughout time and space.

Yet there is also a discrepancy in Luke's salvation scheme. His Gospel begins with a strong emphasis on the importance of Jesus for the Jews, but ends in Acts (26.26–28) by stating that the Jews will remain blind and deaf and the gentiles will receive the promised salvation. What starts out as a kind of primordial Christian inclusivism is quietly transformed into a definite exclusivism. Heikki Räisänen has made this point succinctly: 'Disguised in inclusivist clothing, Luke actually presents an exclusivist thesis: outside Christ, no salvation.'[27]

Räisänen has further pointed out how Luke has been able to achieve his ends through a quiet yet dramatic shift in the meaning of salvation, as his account proceeds. The fulfilment that Israel envisaged is for the restoration of the house of David, as is made abundantly clear in the birth narratives. Salvation is social and it is 'from our enemies and from the hands of all that hate us' (Luke 1.71). But as the Gospel story progresses, another theme, favourite of Luke, assumes dominance: individual repentance and the forgiveness of sins. As Räisänen comments of Luke-Acts: 'Two different views of "salvation" are fused. But it is not said in so many words that the latter vision would supersede the political one.'[28] This gradual transformation of the content of the promise of fulfilment to Israel is traced convincingly throughout Luke-Acts by Räisänen. His conclusion is sobering:

> If God's old promises are fulfilled in Jesus, their content has been changed to such an extent as to be in effect nullified. Luke's vague use of the old language is an indirect indication of this dilemma. In this, Luke shares the problems of all Christian theologies of 'fulfilment' in which the old vocabulary is made to serve a novel cause.[29]

The novel cause of Christian faith may be worth following, as it obviously is for Christians. But, if Räisänen is correct, then the implication is that it is worth retaining a distinction between two versions of Christian fulfilment: one by which Christian faith pursues Judaism's legacy but in an altered key, and one by which the Jewish past is subverted. The former involves no necessary supercessionism; the latter endorses it.

As it is, we know that Jews have often complained that traditional Jewish expectations of the messianic age are not matched by the Christian confession of Jesus as Messiah. Jews harbour a political/communitarian expectation; Christians, on the other hand, have largely been content with the account of individualistic salvation through the forgiveness of sins. Jewish writers, of course, have not been slow to point this out. But, even if the contrast between these two pictures is exaggerated, the Jewish objection to Christian messianism is seldom faced head-on. The Christian response to those objections – that Jesus represents a suffering Messiah – is satisfying to a degree, but only as a basis for *Christian* faith. For Jews, a suffering Messiah compounds the problem and convinces them that Christianity is a different religion from Judaism after all. In Räisänen's terms, the 'old vocabulary' of the promised Messiah has definitely been made to 'serve a novel cause'.

Judaism and Christianity as Separate Religions

Christian approaches to Judaism have undergone significant reversals in recent decades. This has largely been as a result of taking stock in my three areas – through recognizing the follies of 'fulfilment' language, through theological repentance following the 'teaching of contempt' and the Holocaust, and through deconstructing what amounts to a religious ideology of supercessionism. This in turn is giving way to a new phase of Jewish–Christian relations, which is beginning to view those relations as part of the wider issue of interpreting religious plurality globally. However, in order to grasp the opportunities of these developments, it is necessary to return briefly to the negative roots of Jewish–Christian relations.

Jewish–Christian relations, since the Shoah, have concentrated on the roots of the antagonism of two traditions locked, it is often said, into a family quarrel since the destruction of the second temple and the 'parting of the ways'. Yet even to characterize this relationship as a 'family quarrel' could be seriously misleading as a description of what is at stake. Quarrels there have been, and they continue. But it is also reasonable to ask the question: In what sense do Jews and Christians together constitute a 'family' (albeit a dysfunctional one)? As part of Christian identity, it is true that Christians need to understand the origins of their faith-tradition as stemming from the early Judaism of the first century of the Common Era. But what the 'family' analogy fails to grasp is the sense in which Jews and Christians have developed quite different religious apprehensions of life during the intervening period. The context for any newly emerging phase of Jewish–Christian relations is precisely the recognition of the differences between the two communities. For obvious reasons, Jews have been keener to stress the differences than have Christians.

A number of points follow from treating Christianity and Judaism as different religions. First, the older dispute over whether we should affirm 'one covenant' (Christianity participates in the God of the Jewish covenant as a 'sort of extension' of the same religion for the gentiles) or 'two covenants' (Jesus inaugurates a break with the Jewish past but not so successfully that it invalidates Judaism for Jews) rather misses the mark. This is partly because, as we have seen, the evidence of the New Testament, analysed in its first-century setting, does not lend itself to any clear-cut interpretation; and partly because, while the New Testament is indispensable to Christian identity, the exegesis of scripture alone does not determine that identity. Furthermore, in the light of the wider theology of religions debate, talk about only one or two covenants ignores a large part of the world and it therefore seems rather inward-looking.

Much ink has been spilled over trying to resolve the tortuous arguments of first-century Paul in Romans 9–11, and their relevance for Jewish–Christian relations thereafter. Yet, determinative as they have been, these chapters first formed part of the beginnings of a fierce argument about the 'correct' interpretation of the 'old' scriptures. The early church developed its christological model and Judaism developed its rabbinical model: these were two trajectories of religious experience yielding two different religions. But Judaism *now* is not the religion of the Jews who lived 2000 years ago, and Christianity *now* is not the religion of the Christians who lived 2000 years ago. Each tradition has a connection, of course, with their past origins, and part of those connections for each tradition contains an argument with the other. However, those arguments too need to be understood for what they were. Jacob Neusner has made the point that they were arguments conducted through a 'thick veil of incomprehension'. Jews and Christians had very different concerns, asked different questions and came up with different answers. As Neusner expresses it forcefully: 'The two faiths stand for different people talking about different things to different people.'[30] In short, the notion of the *Judeo-Christian* tradition is a misnomer.

Even if Neusner may have exaggerated the extent to which the division between Jewish and Christian concerns was total, given the diversity of early Judaism and the very fluid cultural circumstances of the ancient Greco-Roman world, the passage of time has only added to the incomprehension between two faith-communities. What Neusner thinks was true of the first century of the Common Era has *become* true during the nineteen centuries since then. There is not 'one covenant', nor are there 'two covenants'; there are simply 'different covenants'. And different covenants require to be interpreted as part of a wider religiously plural world.

The second consequence of recognizing Judaism and Christianity as different religions (though with a shared embittered history) is that the dichotomy between the so-called 'uniqueness' of Jewish–Christian relations and its past role as a model for Christian responses to other religious traditions can now be dismantled. Recalling my three areas of enquiry, the Jewish–Christian filter can no longer boost arguments for (a) the Christian fulfilment of other traditions; (b) standing in contempt of other religions; or (c) superseding them. However, to suppose that this filter ought to determine the future of Christian theological responses to other faith-traditions is to continue the contradiction between the 'uniqueness' of Jewish–Christian relations and its role as a model of Christian responses to the wider scene of religious plurality.

Unfortunately, the continuation of this contradiction is common. It can be illustrated, for example, with reference to the proposals of the Catholic theologian, Terence Merrigan. After rejecting Pluralism on the oft-repeated grounds that it fails to do justice to the real differences between traditions, Merrigan then turns to an inclusivist theory. He pays tribute to developments since Vatican II and regards the different religions as vehicles of salvation, which operate as such by virtue of the 'hidden Christ' within them. In relation to Judaism, Merrigan does not wish to follow a doctrine of fulfilment, for 'Judaism emerges not simply as a "foreword" to Christianity, but as a distinctive chapter in God's universal salvific plan'. Therefore, Merrigan thinks that the Jewish–Christian relationship has a major role to play in the dialogue between Christianity and other traditions. He writes:

> What is clear is that Christianity tells a different story than Judaism. What is equally clear, however, is that its story is unintelligible without the Jewish story and that there are themes common to both. In view of that commonality, the Jewish–Christian dialogue is a special case and the progress of that dialogue will have significant consequences for Christianity's dialogue with all other religions.[31]

By repudiating the view that Judaism is a pale reflection of Christianity, Merrigan is able to honour the differences between the two traditions. Yet, once this move is made, why should the Jewish–Christian dialogue remain the 'special case' of all interreligious dialogue? Why not Hindu-Christian or Muslim–Christian dialogue, both of which have had equally tortuous histories? Merrigan's 'commonality' between Judaism and Christianity could well be a case of special pleading. Does Christian faith share nothing 'in common' with other religions?

A further dimension of the special pleading for the Jewish–Christian filter lies in Merrigan's controlling Inclusivism. What binds all of Christianity's relationships with others is the theme of the 'hidden Christ'. Without that, Jewish–Christian relations would remain its own *sui generis* relationship. But, of course, the controlling Inclusivism only deepens the contradiction between the uniqueness of Jewish–Christian dialogue in relation to dialogue more generally. For presumably to inform Jews of the 'hidden Christ' within Judaism raises all of the problems again of supercessionism and the 'teaching of contempt', which the re-establishing of Judaism in Christian eyes as an unrepudiated covenant was intended to transcend.

The third consequence of affirming the distinct differences between Judaism and Christianity is a sense of liberation as representatives from each tradition move towards developing a more positive theological appreciation of the other. But it is noteworthy that where this is taking place it is being pursued as part of a pluralistic framework. From the Jewish side, for example, even a relatively orthodox writer such as Irving Greenberg can affirm the value of the religious other as a 'divine' recommendation:

> Assume there is a divine strategy for redeeming the world using human agents; assume it is the divine will that Judaism and Christianity are together in the world; assume that both are ways of affirming both 'yet' and 'not yet' with regard to redemption. Assume both are true but that both need the other to embody the fullest statement of the coventantal goal and process. What one individual cannot say without being hypocritical or confused, two communities can state as a balance and corrective toward each other.[32]

Greenberg is here speaking of the Jewish–Christian relationship. But his overall picture embraces plurality more widely. For Greenberg, Pluralism is based not only – not even essentially – on the acceptance of human relativity in religious knowing, but on the theological notion of covenant itself. The covenantal divine–human relationship is built on respect and freedom, and that inevitably issues in diversity and difference. As Greenberg says: 'Pluralism is an absolutism that knows its limits. Therefore, it leaves room for other absolute claims and for other faith systems to express themselves in all their power and validity.'[33] Pluralism in this sense is divinely sanctioned, and can be sharply distinguished from relativism.

From the Christian side, enormous strides have been made not only to overturn the historic negative views of Jews and Judaism, but also to reinstate Judaism as a poisitve religion of 'transcendent vision and human transformation'. The veteran Catholic writer in Jewish–Christian dialogue, John Pawlikowski, has helpfully summarized some of these achievements, as follows:

(1) that the Christ Event did not invalidate the Jewish faith perspective;

(2) that Christianity is not superior to Judaism, nor is it the fulfilment of Judaism as previously maintained;

(3) that the Sinai covenant is in principle as crucial to Christian faith expression as the covenant in Christ; and

(4) that Christianity needs to reincorporate dimensions from its original Jewish context.[34]

These building blocks of a new relationship seem to me to prepare the way for viewing Judaism and Christianity as separate religions. Moreover, as gains in Jewish–Christian relations, they are surely best safeguarded theologically within a pluralist theology of religions framework. This is because the tendency in Christian writing will always be to retract from the full implications of the new relationship. For example, even Pawlikowski, who otherwise is committed to 'posit *both* Sinai and the Easter event as equally central',[35] also holds to the Christian incarnational symbol of Christ as heralding what he has described as 'a new depth in the understanding of divine-human bonding'.[36] This has echoes of Geffré's 'certain inclusivism' (see above, p. 45), which retains the doctrine of fulfilment, albeit in mild form. Yet Pawlikowski, along with a great many other Christian writers, has given up 'fulfilment' thinking.

Without a pluralist vision it is hard to see how the residual desire for a Christian universalism which eventually triumphs over all others, first Judaism and then others, can be avoided. But once the integrity of Judaism has been liberated from the shackles of fulfilment and supercessionism, the way is opened for other religions not to be placed, as it were, in the equivalent position of being a forerunner to Christianity.

The Jewish–Christian filter itself has been superseded!

Notes

1 Address to representatives of the Jewish Community of Rome, in Byron L. Sherwin and Harold Kasimow (eds), *John Paul II and Interreligious Dialogue*, Maryknoll: Orbis Books 1999, pp. 72ff.

2 C. Saldanha, *Divine Pedagogy: A Patristic View of Non-Christian Religions*, Rome: Liberia Ateneo Salesiano, 1984, p.161. I am grateful to Jacques Dupuis SJ, *Toward a Christian Theology of Religious Pluralism*, Maryknoll: Orbis Books 1997, p. 78, for this reference.

3 Claude Geffré OP, 'Paul Tillich and the Future of Interreligious Ecumenism', *Paul Tillich: A New Catholic Assessment*, ed. R. F. Bulman and F. J. Parrella, Minnesota: The Liturgical Press 1994, p. 268. Jacques Dupuis has commented about Jean Daniélou, whom Dupuis considers to be 'the first Western exponent of the fulfillment theory', that he has had a 'deep influence' well beyond the impact of Vatican II in the Catholic theology of religions debate. See Dupuis, *Toward a Christian Theology of Religious Pluralism*, pp. 134ff.

4 Geffré, 'Paul Tillich and the Future of Interreligious Ecumenism', p. 268.

5 The Doctrine Commission of the Church of England, *The Mystery of Salvation*, London: Church House Publishing 1995, p. 182.

6 Cf. J. A. DiNoia OP, *The Diversity of Religions: A Christian Perspective*, Washington: Catholic University of America Press 1992, p. 107: 'theology of religions in prospective vein contends that non-Christians will have the opportunity to acknowledge Christ in the future. This opportunity may come to them in the course of their lives here on earth or in the course of their entrance into the life to come'. Also cf. Dupuis, *Toward a Christian Theology of Religious Pluralism*, pp. 389f.

7 David Hartman, 'Towards World Community: Resources for Living Together – A Jewish View', *The Ecumenical Review* 26, October 1974, p. 617.

8 Cf. Richard L. Rubenstein and John K. Roth, *Approaches to Auschwitz: the Legacy of the Holocaust*, London: SCM Press 1987.

9 Jules Isaac, *The Teaching of Contempt*, trans. Helen Weaver, New York: Holt, Rinehart and Winston 1964; cf. the assessment of Irving Greenberg in 'Judaism and Christianity: Their Respective Roles in the Strategy of Redemption', *Visions of the Other: Jewish and Christian Theologians Assess the Dialogue*, ed. Eugene J. Fisher, New York: Paulist Press, A Stimulus Book 1994, p. 20: 'Antisemitism is the most ubiquitous, worldwide, permanent moral infection of human history.'

10 See the excellent little book by Marc Saperstein, *Moments of Crisis in Jewish–Christian Relations*, London: SCM Press 1989 and Philadelphia: Trinity Press 1989, for these references. Saperstein adds in a footnote: 'The association of synagogue, Jews, and the demonic, rooted in the New

Testament (John 8.44; Revelation 2.9, 3.9) would become a topos of medieval and early modern anti-Judaism', p. 66.

11 Consider Augustine's words commenting on Genesis: 'Here no-one can fail to see that in every land where the Jews are scattered, they mourn for the loss of their kingdom and are in terrified subjection to the immensely superior number of Christians ... To the end of the seven days of time the continued preservation of the Jews will be a proof to believing Christians of the subjection merited by those who, in the pride of their kingdom, put the Lord to death', 'Reply to Faustus, the Manichean,' *Disputation and Dialogue: Readings in the Jewish–Christian Encounter*, ed. Frank Ephraim Talmage, New York: KTAV Publishing House 1975, pp. 30–1.

12 Rosemary Radford Ruether, *Faith and Fratricide: The Theological Roots of Anti-Semitism*, New York: Seabury Press 1974.

13 Reproduced in *Catholics Remember the Holocaust*, Washington: United States Catholic Conference 1998, p. 52.

14 See his Introduction to *Faith and Fratricide*, p. 6.

15 Rosemary Radford Ruether, *Disputed Questions: On Being a Christian*, Maryknoll: Orbis Books 1989, p. 56.

16 Ruether, *Disputed Questions*, p. 59; see also the article by Eugene J. Fisher, 'Catholics and Jews Confront the Holocaust and Each Other' and Rosemary Ruether's response, in *World Faiths Encounter* 26 (July 2000). Fisher argues both for a fairly benign view of historic Christian anti-Judaism and for locating the real root of anti-Semitism in a 'pagan' view of biological difference. Ruether's response reaffirms her previous conviction: 'Christianity needs to take responsibility, not only for its previous history of religious hatred of Jews, but also the way these patterns formed the basis for its racial transformation into a policy of extermination' (p. 19).

17 *Faith and Fratricide*, p. 256.

18 See Helen Fry, 'Towards a Christian Theology of Judaism', *Christian-Jewish Dialogue: A Reader*, Exeter: University of Exeter Press 1996, pp. 27ff.

19 Cited by Marcus Braybrooke, *Time to Meet: Towards a Deeper Relationship Between Jews and Christians*, London: SCM Press, p. 28.

20 See the collection of John Paul II's statements on the Jews and Judaism in Eugene Fisher and Leon Klenicki (eds), *Spiritual Pilgrimage: Texts on Jews and Judaism 1979–1995: Pope John Paul II*, New York: Crossroad 1995.

21 David Gordis, 'John Paul II and the Jews', *John Paul II and Interreligious Dialogue*, ed. Byron L. Sherwin and Harold Kasimow, Maryknoll: Orbis Books 1999, p. 130.

22 Cf. Eugene J. Fisher, 'Catholics and Jews Confront the Holocaust and Each Other', *World Faiths Encounter* 26 (July 2000), and responses by Rosemary Ruether and Rabbi Tony Bayfield. Bayfield wonders whether

Christian repentance has been fully offered when the Church retains a remnant of pride when expressing its Christianity.

23 The collection by Sherwin and Kasimow is instructive for noting the parallels between Jewish–Christian relationships and other bilateral relationships. For example, Mahmoud Ayoub (pp. 169–83) has observed that 'when the Holy Father speaks to representatives of the three religions [Jews, Christians and Muslims], he places the three faiths on an equal footing as legitimate paths to God', but in his own writing he concludes that: 'In Islam all the richness of God's self-revelation, which constitutes the heritage of the Old and New Testaments, has definitely been set aside.'

24 Cf. Morna Hooker, *Continuity and Discontinuity: Early Christianity in its Jewish Setting*, London: Epworth Press 1986.

25 E. P. Sanders, *Paul*, Oxford: Oxford University Press 1991, p. 126: 'Israel is simply a part of God's final victory, which will embrace the entire creation'.

26 Donald Senior and Carroll Stuhlmueller, *The Biblical Foundations for Mission*, London: SCM Press 1983, p. 345.

27 Heikki Räisänen, *Marcion, Muhammad and the Mahatma: Exegetical Perspectives on the Encounter of Cultures and Faiths*, London: SCM Press 1997, p. 28. I am grateful to Räisänen's gentle corrective to my earlier optimistic enlisting of Luke's general approach as the beginnings of the inclusivist cause, in my *Christians and Religious Pluralism*, London: SCM Press 1983 and 1993, enlarged second edition, chapter 3.

28 Räisänen, *Marcion, Muhammad and the Mahatma*, p. 51.

29 Räisänen, *Marcion, Muhammad and the Mahatma*, p. 63.

30 Jacob Neusner, *Jews and Christians: The Myth of a Common Tradition*, London: SCM Press, p. 28.

31 Terence Merrigan, 'The Challenge of the Pluralist Theology of Religions and the Christian Rediscovery of Judaism', *Christianity and Judaism*, ed. Didier Pollefyt, Louvain Theological and Pastoral Monographs 23, Leuven: Grand Rapids: W. B. Eerdmans 1997, pp. 95–132.

32 Irving Greenberg, 'Judaism and Christianity: Their Respective Roles in the Strategy of Redemption', *Visions of the Other*, p. 20.

33 Irving Greenberg, 'Seeking the Religious Roots of Pluralism: in the Image of God and Covenant', *Journal of Ecumenical Studies* 34, no. 3, Summer 1997, p. 388.

34 John Pawlikowski, 'Christian Theological Concerns After the Holocaust', *Visions of the Other*, p. 49.

35 John Pawlikowski, *Jesus and the Theology of Israel*, Delaware: Michael Glazier 1989, p. 73.

36 Pawlikowski, 'Christian Theological Concerns After the Holocaust', p. 41; cf. Marcus Braybrooke, *Christian–Jewish Dialogue: The Next Steps*, London: SCM Press 2000.

4

Placing Jesus: The Crunch Issue

The question of how we should interpret the figure of Jesus in Christian faith cannot be separated from understanding his place in the wider multifaith context of our contemporary world. As the Catholic theologian, Roger Haight, has said: 'An adequate christology today must include an account of the relation of Jesus to other religious mediations of God.'[1] Yet the interpretative task faces a confusing array of problems. The interpretation of Jesus has not been constant through history, and the cumulative weight of the new global context of religious plurality appears to add another layer of complexity to the problems.

The issue of the 'uniqueness' of Jesus in relation to other religious epiphanies is central to the debate, together with its backing in the doctrine of the incarnation. For some Christians, Wolfhart Pannenberg's judgement would seem to settle the matter: 'Of course, if Jesus is to be understood as the incarnate son of God, then the claim to Christian uniqueness is inevitable.'[2] Christian faith is God's top choice, and that's that! But there is a lively debate around the doctrine of the incarnation, its appropriateness as the given centre of Christian identity, its intelligibility and its relation to other religions. The concept of 'uniqueness' is not necessarily the only term available for comprehending Jesus and his religious impact.

In recent years a number of arguments have been advanced which make a considerable dent on received christological wisdom. I propose to highlight a number of these arguments briefly and draw out their bearing for the question of the uniqueness of Jesus in the interfaith arena. I shall aim to demonstrate why the traditional affirmation of Jesus as either the eschatological climax of biblical salvation-history or the God-man of Christian dogma are both inadequate for our new circumstances. However, I also contend that there are christological interpretations which have been available for a number of years which allow for a more open approach to the world faiths than has usually been the case throughout Christian history, and I shall end my discussion by drawing attention to these.

In Relation to the New Testament

Studies in the New Testament demonstrate that the titles applied to Jesus in their original setting did not necessarily mean what later Christian tradition took them to be. For example, the formative title 'Son of God' was a symbolic term evocative of the authoritative status of Jesus in the divine scheme of history, not of his divine origins. As Hans Küng has written: 'Originally, the title did not mean a corporeal sonship . . . "Son of God" therefore did not designate Jesus any more than the king of Israel as a superhuman, divine being, but as the appointed ruler.'[3] In other words, the term is metaphorical language.

But perhaps more significant than knowing the historical origins of a term is the commonly accepted insight that the titles attached to Jesus – Son of God, Son of Man, Messiah, Word, Wisdom, etc. – spring from religious commitment and are applied to Jesus as interpretations of his impact. They are not, so to speak, free-floating, bearing the same fixed meaning for each writer and their community's response. In this respect, we may say that Jesus is transformative of a writer's whole outlook. So for Mark, Jesus is the suffering enigmatic Son of Man, confrontational in style and eventually rejected as a 'ransom for many' (Mk 10.45). Or, for Paul, Jesus is the Son of God, whose death and resurrection are said to usher in the era of eschatological hope. Or, for John, he is the enfleshed 'Word' or 'Wisdom', who reveals the truth and grace of God's self-giving love. Each New Testament writer interprets Jesus and his impact according to the community's circumstances, expectations and available theological apparatus for 'receiving' him, with all the richness and limitations these impose.

One major implication of this analysis is that the different

New Testament writers need not be pressed into a mould that became convenient for serving later purposes. That is to say, the tendency to ascribe a 'higher' christology to, say, John's Gospel (because of its 'logos' language) than Mark's Gospel reflects a later agenda, not that of the first communities for whom the Gospels were written.[4] Certainly the later traditions of the Church Fathers may have found the 'logos' language of John more congenial to their theological needs, and appropriated what was in essence imagistic/metaphorical language for their very different conceptual purposes. But to read the New Testament in these terms now is anachronistic. What the New Testament displays is the reminting of symbols, images and metaphors, drawn from the stock of available terms, and their application to Jesus as part of a process of interpreting his impact for the initial generations of the first churches. Even the sporadic incarnational language, found particularly in Paul and John (e.g. Col. 1.15–20; Phil. 2.6–11; John 1.1–18) call for interpretation along these same lines.

For the New Testament witness, Jesus is better understood as the mediator of God's power and presence, rather than as an extension of God's very being.

Finality and Historical Process

The writers portrayed Jesus as the final one from God, the fulfilment of the eschatological promises of God, after the pattern of preparation-fulfilment through Israel's history. In other words, the religious horizon of the New Testament was one of eschatological finality and not ontology. Yet this category of 'finality', which was later transformed into the doctrine of the incarnation, itself has become deeply problematic in a historically critical age. How are we to interpret it? Outside the orthodox Jewish framework what meaning can be attached to the expectation of a messianic figure at the end of history, especially given our knowledge of the history of cultural diversity and our understanding of the timescale of the universe?

The finality/eschatological language of the New Testament – kingdom, resurrection, judgement, Spirit, etc. – does not provide us with information about what is to happen as a kind of religious cosmological prediction. Rather it is stimulus-language, designed to provoke our awareness of the nature of the Divine Life as the ground of all human hoping and living. The Christian achievement has been to interpret the figure of Jesus as the focus for giving rise to this universal awareness. With the application of this language to Jesus, it is small wonder that he was interpreted as God's final agent to usher in the new world, given the cosmology of first-century times.

Critical historical thinking, however, is likely to view history as an interwoven process of cause and effect, stretching into the unknown future, and with little need for a 'final figure' to usher in a 'final age'. As a result of this assessment of history as a 'continuous connection of becoming', to use Ernst Troeltsch's evocative phrase, there has been an immense theological shift towards viewing the whole of creation and history as the *locus* of the immanent presence of God. In turn, this has led to attempts to reinterpret the notion of the finality of Jesus and its successor, the doctrine of the incarnation.

Twentieth-century interpretations of Jesus have been dominated by the imperative to view him more humanly. He is no longer the exception, as it were, to the meaning of humanity under God, but somehow as humanity's goal or 'focus' for that divine–human relationship which has the potential for existing everywhere in the world. So Karl Rahner, for example, could speak of Jesus as the embodiment of perfected free humanity; and John Knox could write that 'the divinity of Christ is a transformed, a redeemed and redemptive humanity'.[5] The language of incarnation was generalized. That is to say, Christianity as an 'incarnational faith' was a religion that valued the physical and the historical as vehicles for experiencing and conveying the presence of God in the world. Moreover, the intention of this type of reformulation was usually to restate classical God-man doctrine. But whether or not the results can be *equated* with this formulation is a moot point.

Myth-Making

My third area of discussion contends that we have moved well beyond the time when we should be able to acknowledge candidly the myth-making tendencies of early Christian doctrine. Beginning in the New Testament and stretching from there through the metaphysical assumptions of the first centuries, these tendencies are exemplified quintessentially in the notion of the pre-existence of Jesus. This was a belief that fitted well with both divine agency traditions of first-century Judaism,[6] and with certain metaphysical assumptions within Greek philosophy that speculated on the explanatory powers of the concept of the *logos* as a mediatorial principle between the heavenly and earthly realms. These two strands of influence merged in the idea of the pre-existence of Jesus, which was the key move in the transition from commitment to Jesus as the biblical 'son of God' to him as 'God the Son', the second person of the Holy Trinity in classical Christian doctrine. The New Testament scholar, John Robinson, summed up the mythological impetus behind this development of doctrine about Jesus: 'To register the conviction that in this man was fulfilled and embodied the meaning of God reaching back to the very beginning, they proclaimed him as his Word, his Image, his Son, from all eternity.'[7] It was the impact of Jesus' whole personality which awakened the sense of God through him. His creative impact initiated a new style of relationship with God, which was summed up by the apostle Paul as 'God was reconciling the world to himself in Christ.'

The critical point to grasp here is that though the language of pre-existence performed a major role in the development of incarnational doctrine, this should not deter us from the frank acknowledgement of the myth-making pressure behind the development of the doctrine. As it is, the notion of pre-existence seldom features in contemporary interpretations of the incarnation, even among those committed in principle to an orthodox understanding.[8] As a belief about Jesus it nearly always robbed him of an authentic humanity.

So far I have made a number of critical observations about the person of Jesus that have challenged some central assumptions in Christian thought. What are their implications for understanding Jesus today? The main implication, I suggest, is that the doctrine of the incarnation is no longer sustainable in its traditional formulation. This claim is not intended to be new. But it is intended to reinforce what many theologians refuse to face.

That is to say: the doctrine of the incarnation has been read into the New Testament rather than out of it; the classical period was preoccupied with myth-making tendencies, around the notion of pre-existence, that are frankly inappropriate for today; and historical consciousness gnaws away at the notion of the unsurpassability of Jesus as a 'revelatory person' wholly different in kind from the rest of humanity.[9] The theologian, Harry Kuitert, has quietly summed up this overall impact of historical critical thinking in relation to the incarnation:

> God-on-earth is first of all an interpretation, a view which people attributed to the Jesus of the Gospels in a particular time and culture, a phase in reception history, albeit one which lasted a long time and left deep traces. Nevertheless, it is a phase.[10]

But we are entering a new phase in history, a phase of global interfaith dialogue. This transition itself is not sufficient reason for interpreting the doctrines of Christian faith afresh, to fit in with some pre-established view of dialogue or Christian theology of religions. But my contention is that the critique of christology already established among many Christian theologians opens the way for a new interpretation of Jesus for a new age. In short, it releases us from the bind I noted in the citation from Pannenberg at the start of this chapter.

The implications of reinterpreting the doctrine of incarnation and its knock-on effect in the idea of Jesus' uniqueness are immense in the context of interfaith dialogue. Already in the earlier part of the twentieth century, Ernst Troeltsch had drawn the general conclusion that Christianity could probably no longer think of itself as the one and only absolute religious truth.[11] Other religions must also be allowed their valid place in the sun. There were other factors about Troeltsch's view which have since become untenable, but in this central respect he seems correct. Again, this does mean that historical consciousness allegedly rules out a priori the possibility of an unsurpassably unique occasion of transcendence inspiring only one of the manifestations of religious life worldwide. But it does shift the burden of proof on to those who wish to retain the absoluteness of Jesus *vis-à-vis* other religions to explain how this is indeed possible.

The Arbitrary or Ambiguous Christ

I wish to turn now to consider the place of Jesus more directly in relation to religious plurality, in order to demonstrate how certain features and ways of speaking of him only compound an already ailing christology fixated on the concept of uniqueness.

The uniqueness of Jesus has commonly been expressed either as a confrontation with other faiths or as the fulfilment of the divine life within them. Neither view takes the above critical approach to christology seriously enough. In so far as the doctrine of the incarnation has functioned as the dogmatic underpinning of the belief in uniqueness, I wish to show how in relation to other faiths it appears either arbitrary or ambiguous.

Let the early Karl Barth be representative of the confrontational arbitrary view: 'It is because we remember and apply the christological doctrine of the *assumptio carnis* that we speak of revelation as the abolition of religion.'[12] Barth was here attacking the concept of 'religion', which in his eyes was synonymous with the human effort to discern the purposes of God without the help of divine grace. The sovereignty of God, Barth believed, transcended all human efforts at self-justification. Though Barth was speaking primarily of what he considered to be the errors of his liberal teachers, and not dwelling on the place of other faiths as such, he nevertheless drew the conclusion that the reality of grace in the Christian story 'differentiates our religion, the Christian, from all others as the true religion'.[13] The neo-orthodox strong distinction between 'religion' and 'revelation' enabled Barth to drive a wedge between Christianity and other religions, and to promote Jesus Christ as the absolute saviour of all.

As often has been pointed out, there is majesty in Barth's proposals. However, there is also an invulnerability that is self-defeating. Once the role of the human imagination in all aspects of knowing, including religious knowing, is admitted, then it is difficult to differentiate so readily between the concepts of 'religion' and 'revelation'. As a device to distinguish between Christian faith and other faiths it is too blunt a device: the experience of religious plurality suggests that the distinction between 'religion' and 'revelation' describes two sides of all traditions rather than delineating the Christian from others. It is possible, of course, to ignore the relevance of that experience, as Barth does. In the end this is what renders Barth's use of the *assumptio carnis* arbitrary. In so far as the doctrine of the incarnation was bound up with the strong distinction between 'religion' and 'revelation', then it is applied in a wholly arbitrary manner. No wonder the claim to unsurpassable uniqueness has often appeared as simply another word for prejudice.

If the early Barth narrowed the incarnation in an exclusive direction then the alternative possibility has exploited its universal possibility. Grounding this view in the Gospel of John's *logos* language, it has been well expressed by the Roman Catholic Federation of Asian Bishops' Conference of 1987:

> In presenting Christ as the 'Word' mediating the mysterious reality of God's presence to the world, John is implicitly admitting the presence of God's self-revelation in other religious traditions. The fact that John presents the Christ-event as an experience which . . . can be identified in the universe at large, shows that the Johannine Church was prepared to enter into dialogue with the surrounding religious traditions.[14]

Whether or not in reality John's community was so open to dialogue as the Asian bishops suggest is a moot point. The bishops could be in danger of applying 'dialogue' anachronistically. However, the theological point is clear enough: God is so committed to the world that we should expect evidence of God's presence through other religious insights. Yet it would be wrong to conclude from this that God's universal presence implies that the knowledge of the divine presence is evenly distributed throughout the world. On the usual interpretation of the Johannine view, Jesus as '*logos* made flesh' necessarily remains the crowning achievement of God's *logos*-presence everywhere.

In relation to other faiths, the problem with this more universal view is that it demonstrates the ambiguity of the incarnation. On the one hand, there is the affirmation of Jesus' solidarity with the human race and therefore potential comparability with other saviours and revealers; on the other hand, Jesus surpasses all others, for in him 'the way, the truth and the life' has been manifest as in no other. This ambiguity is the source of much confusion. For it allows Christians to highlight one side of the ambiguity when in dialogue mode, so that the unsurpassable uniqueness of Jesus is tempered (for example, by the use of terms such as 'decisive') and points of comparability between Jesus and other revealers emphasized; while, on the other side of the ambiguity, and when in theology of religions mode, the eventual superiority of Jesus is retained. What is given in respect through dialogue is removed in the return to Christian (however soft) absolutism when doing theology.

My contention so far has been that both historical and doctrinal critical Christian thought and the added contextual experience of dialogue from other faiths provide overriding reasons for not thinking of Jesus as unsurpassably unique. In the context of dialogue, the uniqueness of Jesus, expressed through the doctrine of the incarnation, appears either as arbitrary or ambiguous in ways that could not have been envisaged earlier in Christian history. The first view allows no place for other faiths and the second assigns them an uncertain place. Factors of arbitrariness and ambiguity compound the already problematic nature of christology in modern debate, once the dialogue between Christianity and other religions is brought into the open.[15]

Deconstruction and Reconstruction

An exercise in the deconstruction of christology can be threatening to traditional faith. Whether one's baseline is the finality/eschatology of the New Testament or the God-man formula of Chalcedon, the results seem to undermine the distinctive identity of Christian faith itself. This is an anxiety that John Macquarrie has expressed: 'I do not think that, if we remain Christian, we can ever escape the fundamental paradox, that Jesus Christ is both human and divine. There are no devices that would eliminate it, short of the destruction of Christianity itself.'[16] However, this is too sweeping and unhistorical a judgement. One could add that a theologically convincing explanation of the God-man formulation has never been forthcoming.[17] The philosophical difficulties of the incarnation concerning how to unite two natures, or two wills, or two consciousnesses in the one person, all derive from the understandable myth-making impulse of early Christian thought associated with the notion of pre-existence. I have not tackled any of these difficulties here, but have concentrated on questions arising from more general considerations.

As it is, incarnational language is highly elastic, as Sarah Coakley has shown.[18] At one end of the spectrum it indicates simply the involvement of the divine mystery with the world process, and at the other, the confinement of its meaning to the technical definition of Chalcedon. If this point about elasticity is valid then speaking of Jesus in the simpler sense, as being 'central in the purposes of God', can be a legitimate starting-point for christology today. My own leaning is away from the Chalcedonian benchmark, for removed from its fifth-century setting it comes close to being what Leslie Houlden has called a 'sheer wonder, a *magnum mysterium*',[19] and Harry Kuitert 'an artificial island of yesterday in the sea of today'.[20]

The reconstruction of christology today begins with historical observation. For our sharpened historical consciousness has taught us how the human response to Jesus has differed markedly through history, and this is a legacy to which any survey of the history of christological reflection will testify.[21] At one level these present a sobering picture of how cultural epochs and settings have created their own version of 'Christ' in their own image. These observations of course raise the acute dilemma of whether or not the figure of Jesus has been used simply as a cipher to meet human aspirations. At this point only attention to the burdens of Jesus of history research can help to alleviate the worst fears of reading our own image into the image of Jesus himself. On the other hand, surveying the pluriform fortunes of christological reflection grants a kind of permission to develop a view of Jesus that is suitable for our own age and circumstances. However, given the dangers of ideology and the potential abuse of the Jesus-tradition for idiosyncratic purposes that are not themselves based on the Jesus-tradition, the christological task is bound to be risky. This will be no less so in relation to the pluralistic environment of today's theological adventure. In this respect, the multifaith context of today's global environment represents simply one latest context in a history of contexts.

If history teaches us that christology has not been simply the repetition of a formula, however venerable, but the interaction of a number of variable factors, then christology is the story of enacted symbolic representation. In this light, Jesus is best interpreted in terms of the language of 'metaphor' or 'symbol'. Jesus is revelatory because of his symbolic value. 'A concrete symbol,' says Roger Haight, ' . . . refers to things, places, events, or persons which mediate a presence and consciousness of another reality'; and it follows, in Haight's estimate that '. . . for Christians, Jesus is the concrete symbol of God'.[22] In a similar vein, though preferring the language of 'metaphor', John Hick has written:

> The idea of the incarnation of God in the life of Jesus, so understood, is thus not a metaphysical claim about Jesus having two natures, but a metaphorical statement of the significance of a life through which God was acting on earth. In Jesus we see a man living in a startling degree of awareness of God and of response to God's presence.[23]

Jesus, in other words, communicates the power, presence and invitation of the spirit of God. Both dimensions – the divine offer of 'transcendent vision and human transformation' and effective human response – are embodied in his person.

One could say it is a high view of symbols I am advocating, one that is both instrumental and representational of what is communicated through it. Objectively, Jesus as 'symbol' evokes the perception that in him a new paradigm of the divine relationship with the world has been opened up. Subjectively, it honours the fact that it is *the Christian* perception that Jesus' Way can be trusted to be what it purports to be, the Christian way of salvation.

It is the nature of the case that key figures in the religious sphere are bound to be invested with symbolic value in a scope that is all-embracing. This certainly happened to Jesus. It has also happened to all other mediator-figures.

What are the implications for the Christian theology of religions of this approach to christology? Using the distinction between Jesus as 'representative' or 'constitutive' of the experience of Christian salvation – a distinction enunciated by the process theologian Schubert Ogden – symbolic or metaphorical christology aligns itself with the former option. 'Representative' christology considers Jesus to be the consolidated exemplar (embodiment, mediation) of universal salvation. Jesus *uncovers*, in the act of faith-response to his impact, the self-giving of God for the life of the world. 'Constitutive' christology, on the other hand, means that Jesus somehow causes or inaugurates what was non-existent previously. He becomes the *origin* of what may be known in various (inadequate) guises elsewhere but is celebrated overtly in the church. The bearing of this distinction on relations with other religions has been highlighted by Paul Knitter: 'Simply stated, as a representative savior, Jesus more readily can stand with others; as a constitutive savior, he stands alone.'[24]

It may be objected that this distinction has no bearing whatsoever on relations with other religions; for the person of Jesus is significant for understanding the nature of Christian salvation only and not for comprehending other goals of the religious life according to other religious worldviews. This, in fact, is the objection of the postmodern insistence on the incommensurability of religious pathways. However, if it is the case that Christian salvation has analogues within other schemes of 'transcendent vision and human transformation' then the objection falls away. What representative christology does is to rescue the iconic value of Jesus from its isolation on the stage of world religious history.

In a bid to sketch out further the potential of representative christology in a pluralistic context, Knitter's distinction between Jesus 'standing with' other revealers and Jesus 'standing alone' is most helpful. Again, he writes:

> To affirm Jesus as *truly* God's Word is to award him a distinctiveness that is his alone; to add that he is not *solely* God's Word is also to see that distinctiveness as one that has to be brought into relationship with other possible Words. Jesus is a Word that can be understood only in conversations with other Words.[25]

By opting for the 'representative-type' approach, Knitter retains his Christian commitment while jettisoning the negative evaluation of other symbolic figures contained in many pre-pluralist formulations.

Of course, much more work of elucidation is required to put

flesh on the bones of a highly suggestive working distinction between 'solely' and 'truly'. Knitter's own elucidations replace the interpretation of Jesus as the 'full, definitive and unsurpassable' ('solely') revelation of the divine with the formulation 'universal, decisive and indispensable' ('truly').[26] The terms here leave themselves open to numerous interpretations, and Knitter himself may not be free from some remaining ambiguities in his meaning. For example, the term 'decisive', in addition to being favoured by the pluralist Knitter, has also been used by inclusivists in a bid to demonstrate the eventual or soft superiority of Jesus as revealer/saviour. Or again, Knitter wants to retain the 'normativity' of Jesus for all peoples and not just for Christians. Yet 'normativity' is used by many to indicate what Knitter rejects in the term 'definitive', a term which generally holds that there can be no other equally significant religious 'norms' in a religiously plural world. But all choices of terms in this debate are fraught with difficulty. Knitter's basic thrust is towards combining the recognition of other religions as contexts for 'saving truth and life', with the Christian centring on Jesus as one who bears a distinctive message and who makes his own challenging difference in the dialogue arena. This concurs with my own stress on the symbolic or metaphorical interpretation of Jesus and his impact.

For many Christians, to settle on 'truly' may seem not quite sufficient as a theological appreciation of the figure of Jesus. Is the 'normativity' of Jesus for Christians only or for the whole world? Ernst Troeltsch, following his extensive global investigations into the relationship between religion and cultural forms, concluded that Christian faith can only be true 'for us', that is, for those who have responded positively to it and mainly from within western cultures.[27] However, it is this perceived limiting of Christian (the same could be said for other universal religions) truth to one section of humanity which seems to undermine the universality of the Christian message. Therefore, Troeltsch's formulation has not won favour. However, notice does need to be taken of his stress on the relativity of knowledge and the nature of truth as interpreted truth. Knitter, along with other pluralists, accepts this factor in modern epistemology. Therefore, he is prepared to admit that other traditions too can be thought of as normative and universally applicable. But what then is the relationship between the 'norm' of Jesus and the 'norms' of other instances of transcendent insight and truth?

The seminal work by Roger Haight, *Jesus: Symbol of God*, offers an attractive suggestion that helps to cut through this dilemma. Haight's suggestion is that in relation to other religions, Jesus functions as a negative norm: 'Jesus functions negatively for the Christian imagination by implying that God is not diametrically other or different or less than the core truth existentially encountered in what is mediated by Jesus.'[28] The 'core truths' of other traditions may be different from the Christian 'core truth', but difference is not to be equated with contradiction. Given that the object of faith is, for Haight, 'absolute mystery', it remains quite feasible for the religions to affirm cognitively different truths and yet not be in direct contradiction.[29] Indeed, this prepares the way for a complementarity of religious truths.

On the positive side of what he intends by the normativity of Jesus, Haight believes that 'Jesus reveals something that has been going on from the beginning, before and outside of Jesus' own influence'.[30] Therefore the universality of God's grace disclosed in the person of Jesus 'opens the imagination to God's presence to the world and guides Christian perception to recognize that what is revealed in him can be enriched by other religious truths'.[31] This in turn leads to one of the primary purposes of dialogue, which is to discern what is involved in the process of enrichment itself.

Haight is clear that both Exclusivism and Inclusivism neither answer the questions implicit in the modern experience of plurality nor heed the message and meaning of Jesus, in so far as he points to and participates in the universal presence of the divine throughout the world. This leads him to 'cross the rubicon'[32] and to embrace a version of the pluralist option in the theology of religions.

Most critics of Pluralism complain that the pluralist hypothesis confuses the different goals of religious commitment manifested in the world religions. But Haight strongly rebuffs this charge.[33] Haight embraces Pluralism as a *theological* option and this is his significant contribution to the debate at this stage.

He demonstrates how it is *qua theologian* that Christianity can conceive of itself as one religion among many without either sacrificing its normative significance as a universal Way or downgrading other religions as penultimate versions of Christian faith. 'The primary argument for the truth and authentic saving power of other religions,' he writes, 'comes from the witness of Jesus Christ.'[34] This is a challenging statement indeed! It may be that by pinning all of his pluralist hopes on the 'witness of Jesus Christ', Haight risks being drawn back into the Christian inclusivist circle. To this extent the more philosophical option explored in Chapter 2 could add further substance to Haight's instincts. It is the witness of people of other faith-traditions and the fruits of religious life that these traditions yield which provide other evidential reasons for embracing the pluralist vision.

Jesus of History

A further implication of the stress on Jesus as symbol and metaphor is that it is of necessity anchored in the historical figure of Jesus. Older, more philosophical formulations tended to float free from any historical moorings. Why, for instance, has it taken until the twentieth century for scholars to recover the historical Jewishness of Jesus as an important component of his identity? So there is no getting away from asking what it was about Jesus that evoked faith from his followers and what that evoked faith might contribute to the dialogue between religions.

The problem with any attempt to recover the historical figure of Jesus is that the Gospel sources themselves are already heavily shaped by the cultural and religious assumptions, social arrangements and arguments of the first churches. Nevertheless, there has been in recent years a resurgence of interest in the historical Jesus by scholars and others alike.[35] The results of this interest show some sharp contrasts in the portrayals that scholars present. However, in general terms, there seems to be a rough division between those who favour Jesus as an end-time prophetic figure of Jewish eschatological expectation and those who portray him as a Jewish peasant akin to Cynic wisdom-teachers of the time. The eschatological portrait goes back at least to

Albert Schweitzer's *Quest for the Historical Jesus* and is upheld in modified form by prominent scholars such as E. P. Sanders; whereas the latter view finds its most obvious voice through the productions of the American-based 'Jesus Seminar' and in particular through its most eloquent spokesman, John Dominic Crossan. A somewhat midway position is taken by fellow Jesus Seminar member, Marcus Borg, who considers Jesus to have been a spirit-filled prophet and religious ecstatic. In other words, he was one who combined prophetic and mystic features, not as an apocalyptic-eschatological figure but as a social critic.[36]

For the non-specialist the variety of 'Jesus portrayals' can seem bewildering. In many respects Borg's portrait of Jesus fulfils the criteria for a truly paradigmatic religious figure, combining spirit-filled mysticism with prophetic social criticism in a holistic vision. Paul Knitter summarizes Borg's four features about the historical Jesus as follows: spirit person, teacher of wisdom, social prophet, movement founder.[37] Perhaps because of these features, Borg's version of Jesus suits the needs of our own times: it can be more readily applied in the present than can the eschatological apocalypticism of the Schweitzer-type view. But we must be on guard against anachronistic readings of the evidence that yet again project back into the New Testament literature answers that suit the needs of our own times. Further, those attracted by the picture of Jesus as a Cynic-type teacher of wisdom need to reckon also with the Jewish critique of this; that it is likely to remove Jesus from his Jewish roots. As Alan Segal says: 'Calling Jesus a Cynic philosopher dissolves his Jewish identity.'[38] For this reason there is more scope in the apocalyptic-eschatological view than recent Jesus research perhaps seems willing to admit. This is not to say, of course, that some of the characteristics of Cynic-type wisdom were not present in Jesus' teachings or behaviour. Most likely they were.

All views about the historical Jesus have to wrestle with the strangeness of Jesus, and in the engagement with this very strangeness itself the modern Christian believer will encounter a critic of his or her conventional culture (religious and secular). In spite of the lack of agreement about the contours of the historical figure of Jesus, through the strangeness we search for clues that can furnish Christian identity with theological trajectories that stir both the Christian identity and dialogue with other religious visions. Many theologians find this in Jesus' announcement of the 'kingdom of God'. Precisely what Jesus intended by 'the kingdom' is a matter of intense debate. However, Dom Crossan's semi-playful comment in response to students, aligning the vision of the kingdom of God with the Hebrew prophets, is apposite: 'I think [Jesus] could have sat down with Amos in the Mediterranean sun, under an olive tree, surely with wine and bread, and they could have agreed that what Amos might have called the covenant of justice, Jesus called the Kingdom of God.'[39] This neatly brings out the prophetic scope of the Jesus of history.

Jesus remains a disturber of social convention, a critic of oppressive relationships, a Jew whose religious experience was grounded in the spirit dimension (for want of a better term) shaped by Jewish history and tradition, a prophet who followed the summons to establish the kingdom of God on earth. A Jewish view this remains, but one capable of application beyond the boundaries of its origins.

In his own lifetime, Jesus enacted the prophetic purposes of God in word and deed under the conditions of one particular setting and culture. As symbol or metaphor and through the symbolic power he accrued, he has also stimulated new possibilities for human responses to those same divine purposes in different cultural settings thereafter. But in the changing history of cultural contexts, and by virtue of its inherent universalism, Jesus-and-the-vision-of-God-to-which-he-has-given-rise is now capable of making its own distinctive contribution to that greater reality of 'transcendent vision and human transformation' which is emerging through interfaith dialogue. Within that dialogue the prophetic witness of Christian faith will need to find its voice. In addition to being necessary, 'being prophetic' has also become precarious, given the complexities of the contemporary world.[40] Nevertheless, it may turn out that through the dialogue itself the prophetic voice will be recovered from the layers of dogmatic speculation that have kept it hidden for so long in the past. Some of these concerns will be taken up again in Chapter 7, in the context of the discussion of global ethics.

Notes

1 Roger Haight SJ, *Jesus: Symbol of God*, Maryknoll: Orbis Press 1999, p. 395.

2 Wolfhart Pannenberg, 'Religious Pluralism and Conflicting Truth-Claims', *The Myth of Christian Uniqueness Reconsidered: The Myth of a Pluralistic Theology of Religions*, ed. Gavin D'Costa, Maryknoll: Orbis Press and London: SCM Press 1987, p. 100.

3 Hans Küng, *On Being a Christian*, Glasgow: Collins Fount 1978, p. 390.

4 See the ground-clearing essay by Leslie Houlden, 'What to Believe About Jesus', in *Connections: the Integration of Theology and Faith*, London: SCM Press 1986, chapter 8. Houlden is one of the few writers to confront candidly the issue of unnecessarily grading the christology of the Gospels for doctrinal purposes.

5 John Macquarrie, *Christology Revisited*, London: SCM Press 1998, p. 78.

6 See Larry Hurtado, *One God, One Lord: Early Christian Devotion and Ancient Jewish Monotheism*, Edinburgh: T&T Clark, second edition 1998.

7 John A. T. Robinson, *The Roots of a Radical*, London: SCM Press 1980, p. 65.

8 John Macquarrie, however, seems to still hanker after it on the final page of his *Christology Revisited*: 'We must not suppose that Christ pre-existed in the sense of waiting like an actor in the wings for the cue when he would step on to the stage of history "in the fullness of time". But it does mean that from the beginning Christ the incarnate Word was there in the counsels of God, and even his humanity, like the humanity of us all, was taking shape in the long ages of cosmic evolution.'

9 Maurice Wiles, in his *Christian Theology and Inter-Religious Dialogue*, London: SCM Press and Philadelphia: Trinity Press 1992 has explored this last point convincingly with reference to the theology of Karl Rahner.

10 H. M. Kuitert, *Jesus: The Legacy of Christianity*, London: SCM Press 1998, p. 129.

11 See his still important final lecture 'The Place of Christianity Among the World Religions', reproduced in John Hick and Brian Hebblethwaite (eds), *Christianity and Other Religions: Selected Readings*, London: Collins, Fount Paperbacks 1980, chapter 1.

12 Karl Barth, *Church Dogmatics*, Vol. 1/2, Edinburgh: T&T Clark 1956, p. 297.

13 Barth, *CD* 1/2, p. 327.

14 Theological Advisory Commission of the Federation of Catholic Asian Bishops' Conferences, 'Seven Theses on Interreligious Dialogue: An

Essay in Pastoral Theological Reflection', reprinted in *International Bulletin of Missionary Research* 13, no. 3, July 1989.

15 A strong exception is perhaps Keith Ward, who believes it is possible to combine Christian orthodoxy with equal dialogical openness to other faith-commitments. But even he is capable of ambivalent signals, e.g. *Religion and Revelation: A Theology of Revelation in the World's Religions*, Oxford: Clarendon Press 1994, p. 280: 'What is present at every time and place is the redemptive self-giving love of God; but its presence is often hidden, ambiguous, and conveyed in many more or less adequate images. The image of the being of God as redemptive love and the purpose of God as participation in the Divine Life is disclosed in the person of Christ and the true form of human redemption is proleptically completed in him.' This seems to me a classic statement of inclusivist christology.

16 Macquarrie, *Christology Revisited*, p. 129.

17 This has been one of the enduring points of John Hick's work. For an exploration of the issues, see his *The Metaphor of God Incarnate*, London: SCM Press 1993, especially chapter 5.

18 Sarah Coakley, *Christ Without Absolutes: A Study of the Christology of Ernst Troeltsch*, Oxford: Clarendon Press 1988, chapter 4, where she outlines six meanings of 'incarnation'.

19 J. L. Houlden, *Connections: The Integration of Theology and Faith*, London: SCM Press 1986, p. 138.

20 H. M. Kuitert, *Jesus: The Legacy of Christianity*, London: SCM Press 1998, p. 111.

21 For example, Jaroslav Pelican, *Jesus through the Centuries: His Place in the History of Culture*, New Haven: Yale University Press 1985. One could add other surveys that account for the mushrooming of christological interpretations in the present across many cultures, e.g. Anton Wessels, *Images of Jesus: How Jesus is Perceived and Portrayed in Non-European Cultures*, London: SCM Press 1990 and Volker Küster, *The Many Faces of Jesus Christ*, London: SCM Press 2000.

22 Haight, *Jesus: Symbol of God*, pp. 13f.

23 Hick, *The Metaphor of God Incarnate*, p. 106.

24 Paul F. Knitter, 'Catholics and Other Religions: Bridging the Gap Between Dialogue and Theology', *Louvain Studies* 24, 1999, pp. 319–54.

25 Paul F. Knitter, *Jesus and the Other Names: Christian Mission and Global Responsibilty*, Maryknoll: Orbis Books 1996, p. 80.

26 Knitter, *Jesus and the Other Names*, chapter 4, 'Uniqueness Revised'. See Knitter's 'Five theses on the Uniqueness of Jesus' in the excellent book *The Uniqueness of Jesus: A Dialogue with Paul F. Knitter*, ed. Leonard Swidler and Paul Mojzes, Maryknoll: Orbis Books 1997, and subsequent various critical responses.

27 Ernst Troeltsch, 'The Place of Christianity Among the World Religions', reproduced in *Christianity and Other Religions: Selected*

Readings, ed. John Hick and Brian Hebblethwaite, Glasgow: Fount Paperbacks 1980, chapter 1.

28 Haight, *Jesus: Symbol of God*, p. 409. The whole section on 'Jesus and the World Religions' presents some of the best argumentation for a theological appreciation of Pluralism.

29 Cf. John Hick's comment that 'the differing belief-systems are beliefs about *different* manifestations of the Real. They're not mutually conflicting beliefs, because they're beliefs about different phenomenal realities', *The Rainbow of Faiths: Critical Dialogues on Religious Pluralism*, London: SCM Press 1995; also published as *A Christian Theology of Religions*, Louisville KY: Westminster/John Knox Press 1995, p. 43.

30 Haight, *Jesus: Symbol of God*, p. 422.

31 Haight, *Jesus: Symbol of God*, p. 410.

32 This was the expression chosen by the contributors to the collection edited by John Hick and Paul F. Knitter, *The Myth of Christian Uniqueness: Toward a Pluralistic Theology of Religions*, Maryknoll: Orbis Press and London: SCM Press 1987, for those who were developing a new paradigm beyond the exclusivist and inclusivist divide in the Christian response to other religions.

33 He explicitly defends John Hick against this criticism, Haight, *Jesus: Symbol of God*, p. 411, fn. 24.

34 Haight, *Jesus: Symbol of God*, p. 412.

35 See Mark Allan Powell, *The Jesus Debate: Modern Historians Investigate the Life of Christ*, Oxford: Lion Publishing 1998, for an excellent overview of the main players in the debate.

36 See Powell, *The Jesus Debate*, for references and discussion of these positions.

37 See his *Jesus and the Other Names*, p. 93.

38 Alan F. Segal, 'Jesus and First-Century Judaism', *Jesus at 2000*, ed. Marcus J. Borg, Colorado and Oxford: Westview Press 1997, p. 66.

39 John Dominic Crossan, 'Jesus and the Kingdom: Itinerants and Householders in Earliest Christianity', *Jesus at 2000*, p. 53.

40 See my 'Precarious and Necessary Prophetic Witness', *Dialogue with a Difference: The Manor House Group Experience*, ed. Tony Bayfield and Marcus Braybrooke, London: SCM Press 1991. See also the writings of Paul Knitter who, in company with numerous Asian Christian writers, has made a passionate virtue of claiming that the prophetic dimension in the service of the kingdom of God is what is distinctive about Jesus' message and person; in particular *Jesus and the Other Names* and his article 'Catholics and Other Religions', *Louvain Studies* 24, 1999; cf. also Aloysius Pieris, *God's Reign for God's Poor: A Return to the Jesus Formula*, Sri Lanka, Tulana Research Centre, second revised edition 1999. See also the discussion in Chapter 8 below.

5

Track Two: The Dialogue Loop

'The literature of "inter-religious dialogue" is already extensive and growing rapidly', wrote Eric Sharpe in 1974, 'but it is not always clear in what sense (or senses) the word is being used, and what are the presuppositions that lie behind it.'[1] Sharpe also noted that the word 'dialogue' had become 'excessively popular' and that 'in many cases it has degenerated into a cliché'.[2] Since then, however, both initiatives for dialogue between people of differing religious convictions and the literature reflecting on these encounters has increased exponentially. Dialogue has become a portmanteau term concealing multiple meanings, depending on the theological and philosophical standpoints of various writers and practitioners and their social contexts.

This chapter begins by offering a working definition of dialogue and then moves to explore what I call the polarity between the 'spirit of dialogue' and the 'theoretics of dialogue'. Most ideas of dialogue entail encounter at least for the sake of mutual understanding, exchange, collaboration, learning, spiritual sharing, theological enrichment, ethical challenge, growth and transformation between persons and traditions. This is a tall order indeed! But dialogue has become a creative means for the appropriation of new forms of religious awareness through encounters that lead to change.

Let me begin with the following reference from Heinrich Ott, as my suggestion of a working definition for encounter through dialogue:

> We probably learn more from each other as human beings, even as religious human beings, and understand God better, when instead of marking off our positions from each other by verbal encounters, we go on questioning together, seeking

together – fully conscious of our differences and yet, at the same time, as if these differences, so to speak, did not exist – what the truth might be.[3]

Ott's reflections are highly paradoxical. He seeks to combine a 'position' with questing and seeking. There is the honouring of differences without letting differences necessarily have the final word. There is commitment to one's own truth with openness to others.[4] These polarities spring from the basic tension between what I call the 'spirit of dialogue' and the 'theoretics of dialogue', both of which are inherent in the nature and practice of dialogue itself. I wish now to explore each dimension in turn.

Evolving the Spirit of Dialogue

Dialogue is not simply the act of human encounter. The theologian, Paul Mojzes, locates it midway between antagonism and synthesis, and this seems correct.[5] At either end of the spectrum of encounter, both antagonism and synthesis are contrary to the spirit of dialogue. Even so, as a *via media* between two extremes, there remains much scope for developing different kinds of relationships that could be described as dialogue. By the spirit of dialogue I am referring to the processes of its conduct, the quality of the relationships it engenders, and the vulnerabilities that lie at the heart of genuine encounter.

But what constitutes genuine encounter? 'When people interact authentically,' wrote the Jewish philosopher, Martin Buber, 'when they move beyond themselves to discover the other person as an equal, they discover a basic reality, a "sphere of between" that links humanity in some greater wholeness.'[6] This was Buber's first criterion for dialogue. It does not dissolve many commitments into one commitment, nor does it collapse openness into sameness and agreement. Dialogue is prepared to risk all – even conversion to the other's stance, perspective or belief.[7]

Dialogue operates in whatever sphere it is conducted – in academic discourse, in arranged encounters between religious institutions (for example, between church, mosque, gurdwara, etc.), or simply as a part of a person's life-praxis. In all of these spheres, the 'spirit' of dialogue proceeds from a creativity that transcends fixed definitions, pre-planned outcomes and final scenarios. This is not to say that dialogue is a totally free-wheeling process, formless or without seriousness. Many of the so-called 'rules' of dialogue that have grown up reflecting the dialogical relationship are evidence of this seriousness and reflect the various settings from which they have emerged.

Among the numerous examples of the 'rules' of dialogue, the 'Deep-Dialogue Decalogue/Critical-Thinking' coined by the Global Dialogue Institute has enjoyed some notoriety (see Appendix 1). These rules give shape to what I am calling the spirit of dialogue. They harbour an expectation that dialogue will make some difference in our overall religious perceptions and practical activities in the struggle to learn more and to change. This is reflected clearly through the example of the Global Dialogue Institute: 'Deep-Dialogue is a way of encountering and understanding oneself and the world at the deepest levels, opening up possibilities of grasping the fundamental meanings of life, individually and corporately, and its various dimensions.'[8] Dialogue, it seems, is fundamental to our being human. It is the opposite of polemic, stereotyping and denigration, and is necessarily informed by the values of respect, trust and empathy.

If dialogue opens up 'possibilities of grasping the fundamental meanings of life', then it will have a direct bearing on the way we do theology. This point has been made by James Fredericks, in an interesting reflection on interreligious friendship as a new theological virtue:

> Friendship is a virtue that recognizes the value of the stranger and equips us with skills for welcoming her or him. Enduring friendships recognize a value in the Other as such. In befriending the stranger, we have not only found a way of taking another human being seriously and rejoicing in what we have in common but also a way of holding in regard what is different from us, what we have not chosen for ourselves for cherishing and living.[9]

Interestingly, according to this account, friendship embraces not simply the common affections between people but also their radical differences, and this is the reason for its potential as a theological virtue in interfaith reflection. In friendship we are taken out of ourselves, rescued from self-absorption, and opened up to other perspectives on life and its meaning. We are potentially transformed. Consequently the shaping of one's own religious identity in a single tradition is not to be divorced from the shared endeavour of discerning religious truth and value across traditions. It is because of the unfolding whole in dialogue that we come to accept that one's own identity is bound up with that of 'the other'. In which case, as Raimon Panikkar has said: in dialogue I meet the other 'in and as myself'.[10]

It is instructive to compare this bare outline of the spirit of dialogue with an account from the world of education. On one model, education is dominantly assumed to be a process of transmission, whereby the teacher (the giver) passes on knowledge as a kind of commodity to the student (the receiver). Much Christian education has functioned in this fashion in the past. While there undoubtedly remains a role for transmission in education, many philosophers of education would agree that this model is insufficient for conveying a more dynamic view of the educational process as a whole. Better is a model that is essentially reciprocal and inclusive of both teacher and student as learners together in an overall dialogical process. In the context of education as a dialogical process for the sake of change, the liberationist educator, Paulo Friere, writes that 'dialogue is the encounter in which the united reflection and action of the dialoguers are addressed to the world which is to be transformed and humanised'.[11] Therefore, dialogue cannot be based on unequal relationships, characterized by the imposition of one's own truth on others.

Filling out his picture further, Friere acknowledges that dialogue proceeds from the virtues of humility (no arrogance), love (no domination), faith (no manipulation), hope (no denial) and, not least, critical thinking (no naivety), and it generates trust leading to change. For Friere, dialogue does not merely repeat the past, but transforms it in a never-ending process: it 'is an act of creation'. The overlap with religious language here will be obvious to anyone.

It seems to me that Friere's insights are directly applicable to interfaith dialogue. The daring remark that dialogue is an 'act of creation' perhaps captures the sense that our existing religious ways, our theologies, soteriologies and eschatologies are to be transcended through dialogue for the sake of that 'greater wholeness' envisaged by Martin Buber. Dialogue does not simply rehearse given positions, but generates its own momentum, extending and challenging previous understandings and commitments.

Many of the hindrances to human liberation noted by Friere – unequal valuing of perspectives, domination of one group by another, assumptions that the world is best characterized by the oppositions of in-group/out-group, pure/impure, saved/unsaved – all have been supported by the religious histories of the world at one time or another. Yet these assumptions are deeply contradictory of the dialogical spirit itself. This is why the notion of dialogue has appeared immensely threatening to the traditional religious outlook. As Leonard Swidler states, dialogue is 'a whole new way of thinking, a way of seeing and reflecting on the world and its meaning'.[12]

Illustrating the Theoretics of Dialogue

If it is true that dialogue represents 'a whole new way of thinking', then it is also the case that no agent of dialogue involves himself or herself in the process, as it were, neutrally or free from perspective. This brings me to the second dimension of dialogue. The 'theoretics' of dialogue embody more overtly the assumptions and goals of the dialogical process itself and therefore bring to the surface the theological and philosophical underpinnings of interreligious encounter. It is probably true to say that much of the burden of theological writing about dialogue has been in terms of clarifying its presuppositions and goals.

The struggle in the churches (and among Christian theologians) for a theological approach to dialogue has not been easy. Rather than give a detailed presentation of some basic concepts that would lend support to the practice of dialogue, I propose to give a brief glimpse into the struggle to formulate what I am calling the theoretics of dialogue by tracing the biographical development of two Christian dialogists – Dr Stanley Samartha (Protestant) and Fr Ignatius Hirudayam (Roman Catholic) – both, interestingly, Asian Indians. Samartha was for a number of years the first Director of the Sub-Unit on Dialogue with People of Living Faiths at the World Council of Churches inaugurated in 1971; and Hirudayam was the Director of Aikiya Alayam Ashram, the Interfaith Research Dialogue Centre in Madras, south India, for many years until his death in 1998. Both men describe the growth of the tension between the search for theological permission for dialogue and the experiential fruits of dialogical encounter itself.

Reflecting on his years (1968–80) at the World Council of Churches, Stanley Samartha describes the gradual acceptance of dialogue as 'a change from "the study of non-Christian religions" to "dialogue with people of living faiths"'. How did this shift happen? Samartha cites at least two major factors: first, changes in world circumstances through the 1960s and 1970s which led to bonds of solidarity between Christians and others in working together for what the WCC termed a 'just, peaceful and sustainable world'; and second, the experience of interfaith dialogue itself. The former thrust the concept of 'common humanity' to the foreground as the controlling consciousness underpinning Christian commitment to a better world; the latter seemed to generate its own momentum without waiting on the theological permission.

The two factors, however, were not equal in their impact. The focus on the concept of 'common humanity' (*humanum*) had the advantage of providing an escape from what Samartha calls the 'post-Tambaram stalemate'. This was the legacy of theological exclusivism dating from the Tambaram missionary conference of 1938, which encouraged theological 'discontinuity' between Christianity and the other religions. But concentration on the *humanum* could also be a distraction from the real task of encounter: as Samartha comments, it was 'an escape route allowing both theologians and missiologists to avoid the challenge of *religions*'.[13] As the concept of the *humanum* is central to the work of the theologian Hans Küng, and has become a guiding principle in the development of a Global Ethic (see Chapter 7), Samartha offers a sobering observation here.

The second factor in the shift towards dialogue in the WCC occurred as a result of the experience of dialogical encounter itself. In 1970 at Ajaltoun, Lebanon, four representatives from different religions – Hindus, Buddhists, Christians and Muslims – met together. Samartha describes the occasion as one of enrichment, going beyond fixed positions, and in which something 'more' than the intentions of the participants and the exchange of ideas was apparent. Borrowing from Hasan Askari, a Muslim sociologist and sufi, Samartha concurred that this 'more' was connected with 'the sense of incompleteness and mutual need' generated by the dialogical process itself. In dialogue, one learns of one's need of the other, not from a sense of inadequacy or even deficiency, but by virtue of recognizing in the other a new source of religious freedom and truth. For Samartha this was summed up by the Hindu participant, Dr Sivaraman of the Banaras Hindu University and a theist of the Saiva Siddhanta school:

> Dialogue between [Christians and others] should not only be possible but even fruitful for understanding man as man (*sic*), and for understanding the deeper truth to which man bears witness, which elevates him to spiritual freedom and to a vision of the spiritual presence in all the religious expressions of man.[14]

In other words, concludes Samartha, dialogue is intrinsic to living one's own faith.

What Christian theology might accompany this new invitation to interreligious dialogue? Samartha himself, in the period of the mid-1970s prior to the publication of the WCC's *Guidelines on Dialogue*, made broad appeals to universalist themes in Christian orthodoxy. These included:

- a view of redemption implying God's commitment to the whole world through the incarnation – 'The incarnation is God's dialogue with humanity';
- the implications of a gospel that places reconciliation at the centre of its proclamation – 'The freedom and love which Christ offers constrain us to be in fellowship with strangers';
- commitment to the work of the Holy Spirit who through relationships with others leads us into all truth – 'dialogue becomes one of the means of the quest for truth'.[15]

Samartha admits that justifications such as these are partially politically motivated, being tailored to hold together different Christian persuasions in a large ecclesiastical organization. Nevertheless, they have been echoed by theologians since and they offer a mandate for dialogical involvement with people of other religions. God indeed has not been without witnesses.

However, in the preparations for the WCC's *Guidelines on Dialogue*, Samartha had already identified the central issue: 'how to state in a theologically credible way the relation between the *universality* of God's love and justice as Creator and the *particularity* of God's revelation in Jesus Christ'.[16] Christology was always destined to become the focus for the tension between the spirit of dialogue, with its disclosure of something 'more', and the theoretics of dialogue that concentrated on granting permission for dialogue in the first place. In later writing, Samartha turned towards the concept of Divine Mystery in order to negotiate the particularity–universality dilemma and prepare the way for a stronger pluralism as the basis for the dialogical endeavour:

> If the great religious traditions of humanity are indeed different responses to the Mystery of God or *Sat* or the Transcendent or Ultimate Reality, then the *distinctiveness* of each response, in this instance the Christian, should be stated in such a way that a mutually critical and enriching *relationship* between different responses becomes naturally possible.[17]

The emphasis on relationship here is important, reflecting an appropriate humility in the face of Divine Mystery and a new way of viewing religious truth in a dialogical age.

Samartha is an ecumenical Protestant.[18] My second personality whose journey illustrates the tension between the spirit and theoretics of dialogue is the Catholic Fr Ignatius Hirudayam. Fr Ignatius describes the move towards dialogue in roughly four stages during his own lifetime. The first stage in Catholic approaches to other religions is described by Fr Ignatius as having been motivated by the familiar distinction between the Christian religion as 'supernatural religion' and the others as, at best, 'natural religions'. This was a theology of the rejection of the other and thus, for Fr Ignatius, failed totally to make sense of the piety of his neighbours. It sustained what he termed a 'dichotomic theology', an intolerable division of the world into Christianity and those religions which exhibited only 'natural gropings' for God; and it was redolent of the colonial attitude.[19]

The second stage in Catholic theology, for Fr Ignatius, accepted the genuineness of religious experience in Indian religion but capped it with the superior truth of Christ in the manner of the theology of fulfilment. The problem with this theology was that it did not match up to its expectations. As Fr Ignatius put it: 'But twenty five years of the study of philosophy, theology, Indology, as well as the vast Tamil religious literature convinced me . . . that there was nothing deep, profound or soul stirring in the writings of the Christian church which could not find a parallel somewhere or other in the vast Tamil literature.'[20] This discovery of riches elsewhere was made possible by the openings presented by Vatican II's inclusivist theology, which was the third stage in his journey. Inclusivism turned to dialogue for a new relationship with people of the Indian religions. But Fr Ignatius learned through dialogue that the religions have different aims that cannot easily be reconciled in a single theological symbol system. Even the inclusivist basis seemed insufficient for the new dialogical world that was being born.

By the mid-1970s the grounds of dialogue based on an inclusivist Christ began to shift and gave way to the fourth stage in Fr Ignatius' journey. He cites an address by the President of the Catholic Bishops in India, Cardinal Picachy, to the Synod of Bishops in Rome in 1974:

> [T]he church in India sees interfaith dialogue as a normal expression of a sharing between religious souls of their experiences. Through this dialogue God calls on each of them, drawing them onward to a higher spirituality and a profounder commitment to Him. We see interfaith dialogue, then, as something good in itself. Through mutual edification and communion men evangelize one another.[21]

This citation indicates the breakthrough of interfaith dialogue. No longer is it something to be argued for but it is 'something good in itself'. Fr Ignatius does not articulate a theology of religions to accompany such discovery, but his stress on mutuality and communion surely contains the seeds of a pluralistic understanding.

Dialogue for its own sake moves beyond the 'theoretics of dialogue' in so far as these have been dominated by seeking only permission for dialogue from the wisdom of tradition. 'Mutual edification and communion' concurs with what Samartha described, albeit elusively, as the 'more' of dialogue. The lesson from experience seems to be that the fruits of dialogue have outgrown the theological apparatus that granted permission for dialogue in the first place.

Dialogue and Common Ground (or not)

Distinguishing the spirit of dialogue from the theoretics of dialogue does not of course entail a total separation between the two. This is to be expected, for under the conditions of mundane reality spirit is never without form, save in respect of ultimate mystery itself. But the distinction does have the advantage of bringing into the open a tension within the heart of the dialogical enterprise as a whole. This basic tension can be expressed through specifying a number of apparent polar opposites. For example, the spirit of dialogue requires that participants in dialogue define themselves, thereby allowing the humanity of religious affiliation to rise above textbook definitions; but assumptions within the theoretics of dialogue can harbour theological evaluations that have the effect of predetermining the place of the other in one's own theological scheme. So pluralists accuse exclusivists and inclusivists of measuring faith by the finality of Christian faith, and exclusivists and inclusivists accuse pluralists of measuring faith by standards external to Christian faith itself. Or again, the spirit of dialogue assumes an equality among participants, but the theologies of particular traditions have traditionally assumed that their own tradition is superior to others, however gently expressed.

Overall, we might put the dilemma like this: in principle, anyone ought to be able to dialogue with anyone else (in the spirit of dialogue); but in reality religious traditions have tended to reserve a corner of the mind, usually unspoken, for their own a priori superiority (in the theoretics of dialogue). Confusion arises by failing to notice dialogue as both a method-process-spirit of encounter and a mode of reflection that seeks to avoid the pitfalls of both absolutism and relativism in the negotiation of plurality.

Is it possible to resolve this dilemma? It is worth setting out two broad perspectives on dialogue, from a Christian point of view, in order to open up the issues involved and point to a way forward.

The theologians of the first perspective preserve the idea that there can only be a tradition-specific approach to dialogue. Christians enter dialogue in order to discover other shapes and witnesses to the 'God who has not left himself without witnesses', no matter how 'strange' these witnesses may seem. These dialogists respect the differences between traditions, even celebrate them. But they find no common ground between them – no common concept of divinity or Ultimate Reality, no common view of the *humanum* or the world, no common experience of religious value. At least we should say that they make no a priori judgement about common ground in the dialogical relationship. Yet they often eschew the language of superiority for they are happy to accept the critical principle that observes how all traditions are partial and historically conditioned in so many ways. Moreover, they know from historical observation that Christianity has made its own contribution to the world's total sum of violence and degradation. Dialogue therefore is a form of relationship that expands one's own horizons of faith and leads to a transformation of outlook without any pretension to stand outside of one's own faith-tradition.

Dialogue may even lead to a measure of complementarity between traditions. The writings of the process theologian, John Cobb, Jr, illustrate the most persuasive version of this position extremely well: 'As dialogue proceeds, glimpses of aspects of reality heretofore unnoticed are vouchsafed the participants. This is not felt as a threat to the religious traditions from which the participants come but as an opportunity for enrichment and even positive transformation.'[22] Cobb considers dialogue to be a process of 'passing over' to another faith, another perspective, and a 'return' to one's own tradition, hopefully enriched, but seldom without profit if the right spirit of openness is present. The fruits of dialogue may even be quite radical, as in his suggestion that it is possible for Christians in dialogue with Buddhists, for example, to 'come to appreciate the *normative* value of the realization of Emptiness', and to 'expand the way they have thought of the purpose and meaning of life'.[23] And normative value, for Cobb, means universal applicability. Both Christianity and Buddhism exist for the whole world, not simply for their own kind; and both Christians and Buddhists should welcome this.

It is perhaps in the area of christology where Cobb sounds more orthodox, though he is far from being unthinkingly dogmatic about the figure of Jesus. Cobb speaks of Christian faith as a circle, at the centre of which is the figure of Jesus. (Other 'circles of faith' will have other figures or revelatory instances at their centres). As Cobb writes: 'We trust the ever-lasting Wisdom because of what happened in Jesus. We affirm Jesus as the centre of our history because in him we find the ever-lasting Wisdom.'[24] It is Cobb's view that as we reach out to others in dialogue we enlarge that circle, without destroying Jesus as its centre and without absorbing others as necessarily inferior versions of the true Wisdom expressed in Jesus. This concurs with much of the inclusivist outlook and is subject to the critique that I offered of it in Chapter 4.

More intriguing, not to say puzzling, is Cobb's refusal to accept Ultimate Reality as unitary. In one sense, of course, Cobb is correct; for the notion of 'one' is part of our human experience and cannot apply directly to Ultimate Reality in itself, which is by definition beyond our human categories. But given Cobb's passionate insistence on the 'root and branch' differences between religious traditions, he is led to hypothesize multiple ultimates. That is to say, the genuine experiences of Buddhists, Christians and Muslims, etc. correspond metaphysically to ontological differences and not simply to phenomenological differences. At this stage in human evolution, believes Cobb, all we can say is that 'the totality of what is, is very complex, far exceeding all that we can ever hope to know or think', and that Christian responsibility in this area leads us to value the universality of many messages.[25] At the very least, says Cobb, the question about a plurality of ultimates ought to be an open question that is subject to the dialogue itself between religions.

Meanwhile, learning to value the universality of other messages will lead Christians to revitalize their own hold on the universalism of the Christian message.

By contrast, let me now outline briefly an alternative view of the theoretics of dialogue, using the example of the Ground Rules of Deep-Dialogue/Critical-Thinking, from the Global Dialogue Institute (GDI), and set out in Appendix 1. This view assumes that dialogue springs from a shared common ground between religions. However, I use the term 'common ground' with caution, as the scope for misunderstanding about this is very great. What it does not mean is that the religions are all the same under the surface of their cultural differences.

Both Cobb and the GDI agree on the spirit of dialogue – of the need for openness and honesty, of respect for the other and equality of participation, of the expectation through dialogue of 'passing over' to another tradition and 'returning' enriched and transformed. However, it is in the explanation of the theoretical principles of deep-dialogue where disagreement with Cobb arises. For the GDI, dialogue uncovers the 'common ground' of the religious worldviews (indeed, all worldviews):

> Deep-Dialogue is grounded in the primal field of Reality itself . . . people have been convinced through the centuries that there must be one originating principle underlying all realities, all world-views, all evolution; this intuition of a primal and global first principle has persisted across all worldviews, including the worldviews of the sciences, insisting that there must be a primal principle as the source of all unity and diversity, a unifying force that both generates and holds together all realities.[26]

Deep-dialogue is more than a technique or a process; its processes (spirit) somehow mirror the nature of reality itself. As one of the GDI authors, Leonard Swidler, says elsewhere: global consciousness is part of a greater paradigm shift in epistemology – away from 'immutability, simplicity, and monologue' towards 'mutuality, relationality, and dialogue . . . as constitutive elements of the very structure of human reality'.[27] In other words, dialogue between religions may not advocate a new religion, but it does invoke a new religious consciousness.

It may seem that the differences between these two styles of dialogue are minimal. Deep-dialogue depends on the willingness to see 'my' perspective as 'a' perspective and not as the 'whole' perspective. Therefore the processes of dialogue are a learning not only *about* the other in their historic and contemporary contexts but *with* the other in a newly emerging global context. This global context is a shared context between worldviews that hitherto we had assumed were necessarily in opposition. These points from the GDI are all in agreement with Cobb. Yet their difference over the issue of 'common ground' is generally assumed to be significant. This difference has been interpreted, in an interesting article by Paul Ingram, in terms of what he calls the 'theology of religions model' of dialogue (exemplified by John Cobb) and the 'primordial model' (exemplified by the American doyen of Religious Studies, Huston Smith, and I would add by the GDI). The former model returns the Christian to his or her own faith-community and thus goes 'beyond dialogue', in Cobb's phrase, in anticipation of a reformulated Christian faith. But the latter's intention is for persons in the dialogical relationship to 'pass over' to 'a primordial point of view that might include our original circle of faith and a lot more. The dialogue never ceases.' Again, as Ingram says: 'The Sacred does not play favorites: all paths *do* lead to the same summit; they need not be interpreted as forms of Advaita Vedanta, and it does not ultimately matter which path one takes as long as it is followed truly and authentically.'[28]

How does one choose between these two models? Cobb's advantage is that he remains clear about his committed stand, generously open as it may be. He pre-empts nothing. Cobb's disadvantage is his unconvincing stand about a possible plurality of ultimates. The GDI's advantage is that it embraces the dialogical relationship without remainder: if through dialogue we come to know truth, then dialogue is the defining matrix of truth and not just a technique. Their disadvantage is that it could give the appearance of not taking the phenomenological differences between traditions seriously enough, and that this leads to a loss in discernment over what can count as true/valid/life-giving religion and what cannot.

For the most part, of course, choice is not required. Dialogue, encounter and collaboration happen, and they lead to change. Even for the strongest absolutist, if dialogue is entered into, a minimum of expectation notwithstanding, then it will make a difference. But it does seem to me that the spirit of dialogue, its inner momentum, challenges significantly any absolutist framework that may be conditioning the encounter. For, if Ingram is correct, then dialogue is what there is.

We have reached a stage where the spirit of dialogue requires to be matched by the theoretics of dialogue. Dialogue in practice (spirit) is outstripping much of the (exclusivist and inclusivist) theology (theoretics) which gave us 'permission' to enter into it as a fact of global reality.

Dialogue is not limited to particular theoretical positions in the theology of religions – and those who complain that pluralists are prone unnecessarily to set an a priori condition on the spirit of dialogue are correct on this point. However, this still does not answer the problem from within the theoretics of dialogue, and it is this area where disagreement is most protracted. For me, exclusivist and inclusivist thinking retain either the whole mind or a corner of the mind for the superiority of Christian faith. And it is this that seems unwarranted once we accept that dialogue really is a 'whole new way of thinking'. Paul Knitter sums this up as follows:

> The correlational model for dialogue I am proposing, with its openness to the truth in other religious cultures, with its view of religions as inherently in need of each other, and with its understanding of truth as many-faceted and in movement, would seem to respond to the ethical inadequacies of the earlier exclusive or inclusive perspectives. If dialogue is an imperative, so is something like the correlational model.[29]

By using the term 'correlational' Knitter intends to offset the criticism of pluralist views that suppose they either forestall the fruits of dialogical encounter before it begins or lead to indifference. But in substance it remains a pluralist view. Dialogue is not a means to an end, but has become the end. This end is not the goal of mere chitchat – which can be left for the coffee break – but the end of mutual transformation for a good that is greater than all traditions in their isolation. This concurs with the theological judgement of Rabbi Irving Greenberg, that 'there has to be a plurality of *legitimate* symbols if the divine intention is to raise humans to the fullest capacities of life'.[30]

Relationships and Issues

To say that 'dialogue is a whole new way of thinking' leaves open the question of how to chart the relationships that are implied by such an assessment. Let me express this by way of what I call the Dialogue Grid:

	Style of Dialogue	Goal of Dialogue	Fruit of Dialogue
Process A	Exchange	Understanding	Discovery
Process B	Negotiation	Tolerance	Acceptance
Process C	Interaction	Communion	Transformation

The processes of dialogue (A, B, C) lead participants from a first face-to-face encounter through a form of parallel existence between faith-traditions, and finally to a state of mutual involvement and accountability. It is a movement between exchanging information, through the negotiation of samenesses and differences and leading to deeper interaction at personal and institutional levels. Similarly, the goals of dialogue may differ according to the style being followed. Much of dialogue begins with exchange of information and the clearing away of misunderstanding and stereotypes of the other. Tolerance is reached when the other seems no longer threatening but in some way comparable with one's own outlook. The goal of communion acknowledges a deeper mutuality that appreciates the other in their strangeness as well as their resonance. The fruits of dialogue might also develop, from discovery through mutual acceptance towards transformation.[31]

Needless to say, this grid does not intend to define the relationships of dialogue according to rigid rules or along neat tramlines. In reality, dialogical relationships often follow a number of patterns on any one occasion. But the circular movement from first encounter to dialogical consciousness as a way of life is what we are called to embrace along Track Two of interfaith relationships. It involves us in learning *about*, *with* and *through* the other.[32]

I have tried to chart a journey that has led to calls for changes in the theoretics of dialogue in order to reflect more faithfully what is transpiring through the spirit of dialogue. This journey applies to every aspect of Christian faith and life. In the following chapters I wish to explore the impact of dialogue in three central areas – theological, ethical and spiritual. But before turning to these aspects it is worth recalling the origins of the dialogue adventure in the modern period, in order to note that many of the substantive issues which preoccupy the dialogue movement have been present since its inception.

From the perspective of those involved in organized international movements for interfaith dialogue, the first Parliament of the World's Religions, held in Chicago in 1893, is being reclaimed as the beginning of 'the interfaith movement' in the modern era. Max Müller, the famous philologist and scholar of Indian traditions, called the Parliament 'one of the most memorable events in the history of the world'.[33] Inflated though that assessment may be, the Parliament was a moment when East met West in an organized setting for the first time on a grand scale, in an attempt to generate a new mood of religious relationships in dialogue.[34]

However, analysis has shown how the social and cultural context of Chicago in 1893 affected the nature of the dialogical exchanges that took place. So Richard Seager, the historian of religion, has written: 'Dazzled by their own accomplishments and charmed by their own magic, Americans were primed to encounter the Asians at the World's Parliament of Religions not in "real" time, but in the realm of America's messianic myth.'[35] The same writer has noted how the centennial event of the Parliament, held in 1993 in Chicago, reversed the contextual deficiency of the first event: 'The contrast between 1893 and 1993 suggests that the national, racial, and religious triumphalism that was part and parcel of the liberalism of the first Parliament has been chastened.'[36] As a result of social analyses of this kind, the dialogue movement is being made aware of the contextual factors which affect interreligious dialogue, factors such as religious representation and the operation of subtle cultural and political power relationships in the dynamics of meeting.[37]

It is not unfair to claim that the lasting value of the first World's Parliament of Religions has been symbolic. Yet a number of themes emerged at that Parliament which have continued to surface in subsequent dialogue endeavours. These are:

- the struggle of 'interreligion' against the 'absence of religion' in modern secularism;
- the need to overcome the historic connection between religious disagreement and violence;
- religion as a liberating and motivating force for good in the world.
- the significance of the Golden Rule ('Do to others what you would have done to yourself') as a potential focus for developing shared values between traditions;
- the problematics of absolutism in commitment to a particular religious path versus the relativism of granting parity of value to all;
- the possibility of a mystical unity of the religions.

If the Parliament deserves its standing as the fountain of institutional dialogue at the start of a new phase in global history, it was important not so much for determining the shape of things to come, as for raising a number of dialogical issues that have proved to be perennial.

Notes

1 Eric J. Sharpe, 'The Goals of Inter-Religious Dialogue', *Truth and Dialogue: The Relationship Between World Religions*, ed. John Hick, Ed., London: Sheldon Press 1974, pp. 77f.

2 Sharpe, 'The Goals of Inter-Religious Dialogue', pp. 77f.

3 Heinrich Ott, 'The Dialogue Between the Religions as a Contemporary Theological Responsibility', *Dialogue in Community: Essays in honour of S. J. Samartha*, ed. C. D. Jathanna, Mangalore: Karnataka Theological Research Institute 1982. The en rules in the citation are mine in order to assist the translation from the German. Further, I would like to make one alteration to this working definition and substitute the term 'Ultimate Reality' for God. This has the effect of creating

space for non-theistic traditions such as Buddhism, Jainism and some forms of Hinduism and Confucianism within the dialogue. It is a small adjustment that does not alter the essential thrust of the main point.

4 Cf. Pieter de Jong, 'Transformation through Interreligious Dialogue', *Inter-Religious Dialogue: Voices from a New Frontier*, ed. M. Darrol Bryant and Frank Flinn, New York: Paragon House 1989, p. 88: 'Commitment without openness leads to fanaticism. Openness without commitment ends in relativism. The answer lies in the balance between commitment and openness.'

5 Paul Mojzes, 'The What and the How of Dialogue', *Inter-Religious Dialogue: Voices from a New Frontier*, p. 200.

6 Cited by Rabbi Rami Mark Shapiro, 'Moving the Fence: One Rabbi's View of Interreligious Dialogue', *Inter-Religious Dialogue: Voices from a New Frontier*, p. 33.

7 Shapiro, 'Moving the Fence', p. 34.

8 'The Dialogue Decalogue: Ground Rules of Personal/Communal Deep-Dialogue/Critical Thinking', ed. Leonard Swidler and Ashok Gangadean, *The Technology of Deep-Dialogue/Critical Thinking*, Global Dialogue Institute, Philadelphia 2000; cf. Martin Buber's second criterion for dialogue: 'This sphere of between is a primal category of human reality available to us through human dialogue' cited by Shapiro, 'Moving the Fence', p. 33.

9 James L. Fredericks, 'Interreligious Friendship: A New Theological Virtue', *Journal of Ecumenical Studies* 35, no. 2, Spring 1998, p. 165.

10 Raimon Panikkar, *Intrareligious Dialogue*, New York: Paulist Press 1978, p. 40.

11 Paulo Friere, *Pedagogy of the Oppressed*, Penguin 1972.

12 Leonard Swidler, *After the Absolute: The Dialogical Future of Religious Reflection*, Minneapolis: Augsburg Fortress 1990, p. xi.

13 Stanley J. Samartha, *Between Two Cultures: Ecumenical Ministry in a Pluralist World*, Geneva: World Council of Churches Publications 1996, p. 40.

14 Cited by Samartha, *Between Two Cultures*, p. 61.

15 Samartha, *Between Two Cultures*, p. 72.

16 Samartha, *Between Two Cultures*, p. 127.

17 Stanley J. Samartha, *One Christ – Many Religions: Toward a Revised Christology*, Maryknoll: Orbis Press 1991, p. 86.

18 Actually, he describes himself as 'Hindu by culture, Christian by faith, Indian by citizenship, and ecumenical by choice', *Between Two Cultures*, p. 161.

19 Ignatius Hirudayam, 'My Spiritual Journey through the Highways and Byways of Interreligious Dialogue', *Inter-Religious Dialogue: Voices from a New Frontier*, p. 55.

20 Hirudayam, 'My Spiritual Journey', p. 55.

21 Hirudayam, 'My Spiritual Journey', p. 55.

22 John Cobb, Jr, 'Beyond Pluralism', *Transforming Christianity and the World: A Way Beyond Absolutism and Relativism*, edited and introduced by Paul Knitter, Maryknoll: Orbis Press 1999, p. 66.

23 Cobb, 'Beyond Pluralism', p. 67.

24 'Toward a Christocentric Catholic Theology', *Transforming Christianity and the World*, p. 79.

25 'Christian Universality Revisited', *Transforming Christianity and the World*, p. 135.

26 Leonard Swidler and Ashok Gangadean, *The Technology of Deep-Dialogue/Critical Thinking*.

27 Swidler, *After the Absolute*, p. 6.

28 Paul O. Ingram, 'Two Western Models of Interreligious Dialogue', *Journal of Ecumenical Studies* 26, no. 1, Winter 1989, pp. 8–28.

29 Paul F. Knitter, *Jesus and the Other Names: Christian Mission and Global Responsibility*, Maryknoll: Orbis Press 1996, p. 34.

30 Irving Greenberg, 'Judaism and Christianity: Their Respective Roles in the Strategy of Redemption', *Visions of the Other: Jewish and Christian Theologians Assess the Dialogue*, ed. Eugene J. Fisher, New York: Paulist Press, A Stimulus Book 1994, p. 24, italics mine. Cf. the experience of Rabbi Rami Mark Shapiro: 'We need only be present, fully and passionately there, offering through silence or words our bit of wisdom to the unfolding whole', 'Moving the Fence', p. 34.

31 The Global Dialogue Institute describe seven stages of 'deep-dialogue' in a most careful description of how dialogue might proceed. See Swidler and Gangadean, *The Technology of Deep-Dialogue/Critical Thinking*.

32 Cf. Leonard Swidler, John B. Cobb, Jr, Paul F. Knitter, Monica K. Hellwig (eds), *Death or Dialogue?: From the Age of Monologue to the Age of Dialogue*, London: SCM Press and Philadelphia: Trinity Press 1990.

33 F. Max Müller, 'The Real Significance of the Parliament of Religions', *Arena* 11, December 1894, pp. 1f.

34 See Marcus Braybrooke, *Pilgrimage of Hope: One Hundred Years of Global Interfaith Dialogue*, London: SCM Press 1992.

35 Richard Hughes Seagar, 'The World's Parliament of Religions, Chicago, Illinois 1893: America's Coming of Age', Ph.D. thesis, Harvard University, 1986.

36 Richard Hughes Seagar, 'The Two Parliaments, the 1893 Original and the Centennial of 1993: A Historian's View', in *The Community of Religions: Voices and Images of the Parliament of the World's Religions*, ed. Wayne Teasdale and George Cairns, New York: Continuum 1999, p. 30.

37 Cf. Paul F. Knitter, 'Pluralism and Oppression: Dialogue Between the Many Religions and the Many Poor', in *The Community of Religions*.

6

Defending Pluralism

Taking the implications of dialogue seriously as a process and context for 'a new way of thinking' entails, in David Tracy's celebrated line, that 'dialogue is no longer a luxury but a theological necessity'.[1] That message is beginning to filter through into Christian theological circles slowly, as can be witnessed by a number of recent theological works written consciously from a dialogical perspective.[2]

Yet more is at stake than minor tampering with some minor aspects of the Christian tradition. If dialogue, in its theological aspect, aims to stimulate mutual learning and to promote shared seeking towards new horizons of truth then the heartlands of Christian theology as a whole will be profoundly affected. We are in the midst of a paradigm shift that is at least beginning to be noticed candidly. So the International Theological Commission of the Vatican acknowledges the implications of the dialogical world: 'How can one enter into an interreligious dialogue, respecting all religions and not considering them in advance as imperfect and inferior, if we recognize in Jesus Christ and only in him the unique and universal Saviour of mankind?'[3] This locates the problem in christological terms, and it is indeed in the area of christology where the dilemma is felt most acutely, at least in the western churches. Whether or not the Commission gives a satisfactory answer I shall examine shortly. But the question it asks delineates as sharply as possible what is at stake.

Yet some might think that the Theological Commission's question is misleading. There is a proper distinction between theology and dialogue that needs to be maintained for the health of both activities. This objection has some force. However, if there is an obvious and necessary difference between the two activities there is also a firm link. For the experience of dialogue (Track Two) forms part of the data for reflection in the theology of religions (Track One). This theology is not simply about interpreting the texts and histories of others, as it were at arm's length. But it approaches these texts and histories as living experiences through their embodiment in people of other faith-traditions in the present.[4] It may be that permission for dialogue is to be found in the universalizing thrust of some Christian texts and patterns of thought. Under the momentum of dialogue, theology itself is open to revision.

There seems no way of avoiding the observation that the inconsistency between theology and dialogue is acute. This chapter examines this inconsistency or gap between the acceptance of the rhetoric of dialogue by theologians, missiologists and churches and their residual failure to take seriously the full theological impact of the assumptions and consequences of that rhetoric. I shall begin by setting out some examples of the gap as I see it; then I shall reiterate the benefits of a pluralist theology of religions as a best solution to the problem to date, discussing some critical voices along the way.

Examples of Inconsistency

A classic statement which attempts to mediate between theology of religions and dialogue between religions is the Catholic document *Dialogue and Proclamation*.[5] This document is clear that dialogue is not simply polite exchanges of information:

> The foundation of the Church's commitment to dialogue is not merely anthropological but primarily theological. God, in an age-long dialogue, has offered and continues to offer salvation to humankind. In faithfulness to the divine initiative, the Church too must enter into a dialogue of salvation with all men and women.

> [Interreligious dialogue] reaches a much deeper level, that of the spirit, where exchange and sharing consist in a mutual witness to one's beliefs and a common exploration of one's respective religious convictions.

> Sincere dialogue implies, on the one hand, mutual acceptance

of differences, or even of contradictions, and on the other, respect for the free decision of persons taken according to the dictates of their conscience.

In other places, Pope John Paul II makes clear his own deep commitment to dialogue: 'Through interreligious dialogue we are able to bear witness to those truths which are the necessary point of reference for the individual and for society: the dignity of each and every human being, whatever his or her ethnic origin, religious affiliation, or political commitment.'[6] The themes of the spirit of dialogue are all present here: religious commitment, mutuality, common search, accepting differences and potential contradictions, respect for religious otherness in conscience. They confirm what the papal encyclical *Redemptoris Missio* had proposed in 1990: 'Dialogue does not originate from tactical concerns or self-interest, but is an activity with its own guiding principles, requirements and dignity.'[7]

If no one should doubt the commitment to dialogue represented by these documents, what is the relationship of this commitment to the theology of religions? The answer is contained in the summation phrase: 'interreligious dialogue is an integral element of the Church's evangelizing mission'.[8] In other words, the whole context makes it crystal clear that dialogue is subject to the controls of a theology of religions which believes Christianity to be the final truth. Concurring with the broad concept of the *missio dei*, dialogue is held to be one dimension of a complex set of 'mission' activities and reflective processes. Therefore it is no accident that the following statements give the impression of being at odds with the spirit of dialogue: '[There] is but one plan of salvation for humankind, with its center in Jesus Christ, who in his incarnation "has united himself in a certain manner to every person"';[9] and 'In dialogue Christians and others are invited to deepen their religious commitment, to respond with increasing sincerity to God's personal call and gracious self-gift which, as our faith tells us, always passes through the mediation of Jesus Christ and the work of his Spirit.'[10]

Again, in his encyclical *Redemptoris Missio*, the Pope states with exemplary clarity how the integrity of dialogue is compromised by the a priori of theology: 'Dialogue should be conducted and implemented with the conviction that the church is the ordinary means of salvation and that she alone possesses the fullness of the means of salvation.'[11] It needs to be said that these official Catholic pronouncements intend no deception. Their internal logic derives from Inclusivism, whereby the values inherent in other traditions, although prized in themselves for those who follow them, nevertheless remain 'unfulfilled' in the light of the incarnation of Christ. My point here, however, has been to highlight a basic difficulty: once the dialogical turn has been accepted, continuing the old rhetoric of 'fullness of the means of salvation' undercuts the assumptions and aspirations of dialogue itself.

It is worth noting that the same observation has been made from outside the Christian faith-commitment by members of other traditions. In a very telling analysis, Jewish, Muslim and Buddhist representative theologians and philosophers have examined papal statements that are supportive of dialogue and demonstrated a remarkable almost near agreement in their responses.[12] On the one hand, they applaud the openness of the Pope when he speaks dialogically – the basis for which might be human rights and respect for common humanity, or a sense of transcendental spirit at the heart of all human cultures, or the need for collaboration to combat the distortions of materialism. Yet, on the other hand, they express grave disappointment when he continues to express Christian absolutism in his theology of religions. The mutuality inherent in dialogical relationships is eclipsed when it comes to theological reflection.

This inconsistency between theology and the practice of dialogue is problematic not only for Christianity but also for all religions. As David Gordis points out: 'Pluralism means coming to terms with the truth claims of the other and an adjustment of one's own claims to truth. Pluralism requires a degree of "epistemological modesty," and is uncommon in the historical record of all religions and in the doctrines of virtually all faiths.'[13] Gordis is not arguing for a particular theory of pluralism. What he is forcing into the open, however, is the recognition that the whole context, spirit and thrust of dialogical relation-ships cannot be supported by a theology of religions based on absolutist convictions. By definition, absolutist convictions are opposed to 'epistemological modesty'.

Dialogue and Pluralism

I have explored some angles of the Catholic discussion of the inconsistency between dialogical practice and theological affirmations, but a similar account could have been given from Protestant or Orthodox literature.[14] If the ecclesiastical solutions are not convincing, what can be said for pluralist solutions in the theology of religions as a response to the context of dialogue? Paul Knitter sharpens the notion of 'epistemological modesty' by insisting that a genuine relationship between people of faith-traditions is only possible on the basis of 'a give and take which really flows, equally, both ways' and where 'both sides are expected and are able to give and receive, speak and listen, teach and learn, challenge and be challenged'.[15] But is the surrender of the language of finality necessary for such a dialogue? Pluralists say that it is.

Giving up finality, however, is not the same as accepting without question every dimension, belief and value of any religion in the dialogue. As Knitter explains further:

> [Pluralists] do not mean that all religions, in their nature as religions and their present condition, are equally valid in all they teach or do, or really say the same thing. Rather, pluralists are stating that in order to have a real dialogue, all the religious participants have to have equal rights.[16]

Clearly Knitter is using the language of 'equal rights' in a highly specific sense here. Upholding rights in the dialogue context is not simply a matter of granting a participant in dialogue the right to participate without intimidation. When one partner (or both) retains the 'fullness' of religious truth Knitter contends that faithfulness to the equality of rights – 'to teach and to learn' – has been breached. Also, it is hard to imagine how the language of 'fullness' can facilitate a 'giving and receiving' other than of a fairly superficial kind. Therefore, the pluralist believes that the best case for underpinning and pursuing interreligious dialogue involves a combination of 'epistemological modesty' and 'equal rights' between faith-traditions.

Pluralism, as a hypothesis in the theology of religions, envisages that faith-traditions which have sustained a long period of 'transcendent vision and human transformation' contribute to a wider picture of religious truth than can be apprehended by one tradition alone. So Wilfred Cantwell Smith avers: 'Each tradition, being finite, has even at its best drawn attention to some facets only of the transcendence to which humanity is open.'[17] Put like that, this still leaves rather vague the meaning of the term 'transcendence'. Cantwell Smith's observations are made as a historian of religion. What is needed is a philosophical means by which the specificities of 'transcendence', found in the different traditions are honoured while their 'facets' as part of a greater whole are brought into relationship more clearly. John Hick's distinction between the 'noumenon' of Ultimate Reality and the 'phenomena' of the human-historical apprehensions of ultimacy in the religions provides one means for clarifying how this might be achieved. In dialogue, participants will be aware that Ultimate Reality will be possessed of a richness which can sustain different manifestations of the fullness of its hidden truth. Furthermore, given the fact of human finitude and our humanly limited perceptive capacities, dialogue will yield much to argue about, much to 'challenge and be challenged' by, much to be fascinated by and repulsed by, in a process which is likely to work towards complementarity between traditions.

Critical Voices

The tie-up between the pluralist hypothesis and the practice of dialogue has, for many theologians and practitioners, been made too hurriedly. Critics of Pluralism contend that, viewed simply as a process of encounter, interreligious dialogue has no need of the language of 'equal rights' and 'epistemological modesty'. All that is required is the willingness to engage in the process in respect, readiness to listen and without misrepresentation. Absolutists may believe that their version of the truth is the final one, but this need not entail that there is nothing to learn from elsewhere. Dialogue, the argument continues, does not forswear the honest expression of convictions; indeed, it thrives on participants remaining honest about differences, disagreements and incompatibilities between religions.

The pluralist's concern, however, is simply that if a corner of the mind is reserved for superiority then the dialogue is unlikely to be fully open. But absolutist theologians who believe that fully open dialogue does remain possible generally advance their case by first launching their attack on Pluralism. Therefore, I shall list and respond to a number of critical issues in order to strengthen the pluralist case as the best framework for promoting open dialogue. I shall conclude with some remarks about complementarity between faith-traditions.

There are three essential critical arguments raised against Pluralism:

(a) Pluralism has pretensions to occupy an Olympian neutral position beyond the positions of all traditions and therefore becomes another absolutist position that turns out to be a form of thinly religiously disguised secularism.

(b) Pluralism does not take diversity with full seriousness and it destroys true dialogue by removing the grounds for encountering real differences and disagreements between religions.

(c) Pluralism fails to see the potential within orthodox Christian faith for meeting the new challenges of pluralism, and in particular for negotiating creatively the tension between theology and dialogue.

Although they are by no means exhaustive, these charges against Pluralism are serious accusations. Let me consider each objection in turn.

First, for over a decade the objection has been raised, from a number of angles, that pluralist views embody what has been called 'the myth of the neutral observer'.[18] From a political angle, it has been claimed that it is no accident that pluralist theologies are emerging at the same time as western interests are seeking to mould the 'unity' of our 'one world' for its own economic-political interests through the phenomenon known as 'globalization'. 'Free economics' and 'free exchange of ideas' (dialogue, no less), it is said, are analogously related component parts of a neo-liberal ideology that seeks to dominate the world in all aspects of influence and control. This includes the production not only of goods and services but also of knowledge. To this end, the promotion of dialogical harmony between religions functions as an unspoken means for dampening any potential dissent from the dominant 'globalizing' model.[19]

What can be said in response to this critique? It seems to me that while it is valid as a reminder of the global political context(s) in which interreligious dialogue is taking place, such a critique makes its impact by turning all intellectual activity into a form of political discourse. There is, of course, a political relationship within all discourse, including interreligious discourse. If it were true, however, that pluralist theologies of religion show no capacity for developing criteria for discrimination between different values and beliefs, then the critique would be considerable. The critique may point to a potential weakness in pluralist positions, but it is by no means obvious that Pluralism is merely a function of western-style imperialism. Campaigners for global justice and equality can be found on all points of the spectrum of views dealing with the theology of religions. From a pluralist perspective, moreover, there are those who have made the demand for global justice central to their model of interreligious relationships and pluralist thinking.[20] As these issues arise perhaps more pertinently within the discussion about a Global Ethic, I therefore propose to postpone further discussion of them until Chapter 7.

The philosophical form of the objection has been raised incisively by Gavin D'Costa, who complains that Hick's version of Pluralism substitutes for the Christian understanding of God at the centre of reality 'a form of ethical agnosticism', which is essentially 'modernity's god'.[21] Preparing the way for this objection to Hick is D'Costa's embrace of the so-called postmodern criticism of the eighteenth-century European Enlightenment. Critics of the Enlightenment claim that the latter's pretensions to universalist reason, exemplified supremely by a figure such as Immanuel Kant, tamed the specific claims of religious ontology and reduced religious commitment to universal ethical principles. (Witness the two principles above of 'epistemological modesty' and 'equal rights'!). Yet the critique of Enlightenment reason has demonstrated that Enlightenment reason is itself as much a tradition-specific product as any other intellectual movement or religion. Therefore the 'grand narrative' of the Enlightenment can be seen for what it is: one narrative among others. D'Costa views Pluralism as a form of Enlightenment 'grand narrative' in religious guise, and as such fails when measured against the postmodern critique of the Enlightenment.

D'Costa speaks with particular force against Hick's Kantian distinction between the noumenal Real *an sich* and the phenomenal 'images' of the Real known and experienced within the specific religious traditions of global human history in varied forms. This is the centrepiece of Hick's hypothesis and the main give-away of Hick's capitulation to secular modernity, as far as D'Costa is concerned. It amounts to a form of exclusive intolerance, the very opposite of its intention: 'Hick's Enlightenment exclusivism stems from his Kantian epistemology and establishes his ontological agnosticism.'[22]

It seems to me that D'Costa, while raising genuine issues, has polemically overplayed his hand. Hick has repeatedly said that he is using only one strand of Kant's giant *corpus* and applying it to the problems of interpreting religious plurality. One may accept the validity of the challenge posed by the postmodern critique of the Enlightenment – that the dream of formulating an all-embracing form of universal reason has been mistaken – without thereby dismissing many of the Enlightenment's valid insights. Similarly, one need not accept the whole of Kant's philosophy in order to see the truth of some of his proposals. Hick does not in fact repeat Kant's religious epistemology, as D'Costa seems to think, but borrows from his central insights concerning the active role of the human mind in perceiving and conceptually structuring our experience of reality. Applying this to religious experience, Hick is then able to account for the significant variations between the religious traditions concerning their basic outlooks and developed theologies and philosophies, while retaining a 'hidden common ground' in the transcendent Real.

The further point to make here is that the pluralist position is a religiously motivated interpretation and is not a form of secular modernity. Hick accepts the basic cognitive character of his Christian conviction and experience which, in turn, is confirmed by the moral and spiritual fruits it yields. He then applies the same ground rules to other traditions arguing inductively to formulate the hypothesis of 'an ultimate divine reality which is being differently conceived, and therefore differently experienced, from within the different religio-cultural ways of being human'. He further explains: 'This is an hypothesis offered to explain, from a religious as distinguished from a naturalistic point of view, the facts described by the historians of religion.'[23] Of course, it may be that the laudable intention to establish a religiously motivated pluralist interpretation of plurality cannot avoid being subsumed by the generally secular or at least religiously reductionist stance of the Enlightenment, as the critics see it; and this too seems to be part of the burden of D'Costa's critique. Tackling this takes us to the next section of the defence of Pluralism within a dialogical framework of seeking religious truth.

The second accusation often made against pluralists is that they do not take with full seriousness the vast differences between the religions. Religious traditions not only arise from particular historical circumstances but have spawned different theologies and eschatologies, in short, different religious goals and aims. Therefore, my own formulation 'transcendent vision and human transformation', John Hick's 'transformation from self-centredness to centring in the Real', and even Paul Knitter's recommendation of 'eco-human suffering' as the rallying point for interreligious dialogue could each be accused of the sin of what is known, in the ugly term, as 'homogenization'. As the Catholic writer, J. A. DiNoia, has expressed it: 'To say that religions aim at "ultimacy" or at "reality" is to state an aim of such generality as to fail entirely to describe what actually transpires in religious communities.'[24] It is alleged that generalized formulations destroy – perhaps unwittingly, but nevertheless drastically – the particular colours and forms of life which define the differences between traditions. In turn, the critique continues, the philosophical effect of such generic formulae is to loosen the referential value of the particularities of specific traditions and thereby drain the religions of their power which derives precisely from their specific differences.

What can be said in response to these charges? Broadly speaking, let me offer two responses, both of which point out how the types of observations made by DiNoia represent a failure to grasp the subtlety of the pluralist hypothesis. First, DiNoia's complaint seems based on the choice: *either* religious claims are real/true and cognitively referential in relation to ultimate truth *or* they are culturally pragmatically referential only. Pluralism, however, refuses that choice. It does so on the grounds that truth reference in religious affirmation is necessarily indirect. Religious truth, we have come to see, is intrinsically linked to communities, cultures and histories. Its language is symbolic and perspectival, and has evolved according to its use in particular cultural contexts and religious-imaginative frameworks. If this is accepted, as it now is by most philosophers of religion, then there is a prima facie case for not subscribing to any simple choice between reference or not-reference in religious affirmations. DiNoia also accepts that cultural factors determine to a large measure the religious perception of truth. But he sees this, in postmodern fashion, as an indication of near incommensurability in relationships between the religions. This seems to me to be unnecessarily pessimistic about the nature of religious truth itself.

Of course, being reminded of the indirect nature of religious language (with its interwoven criss-crossing of different types of language – metaphor, symbol, analogy, myth, history etc.) does not solve the problem of how such radical difference between faith-traditions might be related in a higher transcendence. Moreover, the use of analogies do not always illuminate the situation as we might hope. For example, the famous Buddhist parable of the blind men who catch hold of only one part of an elephant and declare its identity accordingly – as a brush (tail) or a plough (trunk), and so on[25] – or the analogy of the 'many roads up the mountain leading to the same summit', both suffer from the problem that they rely on an outsider's viewpoint which is able to identify the true picture from the partial pictures of the blind men or of the mountain climbers. It is precisely this outside viewpoint which is lacking in our human experience.[26] We are all insiders! Does this mean therefore that, even if the point about the indirectness of religious language is accepted among religious philosophers, DiNoia's assessment of pluralist solutions must be correct after all? Let me now turn to the second failure of the DiNoia type observation in order to demonstrate further the viability and necessity of the pluralist option.

A strong defence of Pluralism has been made by pointing out the subtlety of its combination in both pragmatist and cognitivist views of religious language. By subscribing to the usual view that these two explanations of religious language are essentially rivals, DiNoia has been led to see only an either/or possibility. The choice goes: on the one hand, if the religions are pragmatic contexts for leading a 'spiritual life' – for pursuing 'transcendent vision and human transformation' – then Pluralism has in effect yielded to secularism by virtue of substituting an ethical for a theological view of religious commitment (this is a major criticism of D'Costa); on the other hand, if religious belief is intended as cognitive, then the varying world religious affirmations remain ultimately incompatible.

But this usual opposition fails to note how the two types of interpretation of religious language can coexist in the same model. So Sumner Twiss has pointed out how Hick employs a pragmatic-grammatical view of religious language when he is describing the religions severally as 'contexts of salvation/ liberation', which function to transform human life and are judged by their spiritual and moral fruits; and a critical realist-cognitivist view of religious language when he is explaining their pluralist orientation on Ultimate Reality, this being necessary for a properly *religious* interpretation of plurality. Twiss describes this two-tiered approach as a (legitimate) hybrid account by which: 'The diverse religions are conceptualized as *cultural-linguistic grammars* or idioms for engaging in soteriologically oriented forms of religious life that ultimately *refer* to one radically transcendent reality.'[27] That a meta-theory explaining the different faith-traditions as different responses to 'the Real' does not spring directly from the traditions themselves is no objection therefore to its legitimacy. 'It is to be expected,' says Twiss, 'that a higher-order theoretical account would identify deeper (and perhaps common) explanatory factors that the more limited traditional perspectives would not have in view.'[28] On a pluralist model, the differences between the religions are neither collapsed nor are they held apart as being wholly incommensurable. It is the distinction between and combined employment of two views of religious language – pragmatic and critical realist – which enables the pluralist hypothesis to function as an explanation for how component parts of a religiously motivated hypothesis about religious plurality fits together.

Much more than pointing out the subtle use of different interpretations of religious language is involved in the pluralist case. My point here has been to show how Pluralism explains how the religions are respected in their radical differences without capitulating to either a non-referential view of religious language or the pessimism of incommensurability between traditions.

There is one respect, however, in which Pluralism does not leave the religions intact, and that is in their claims to be the absolute and universal truth. It is holding on to this belief that is said to militate against any pluralist interpretation of global religious history. But is it possible to enter dialogue with a genuine sense of one's own religious identity and simultaneously think of that identity in a de-absolutized manner? This brings me to the third aspect of the objections to Pluralism.

A third objection to Pluralism considers that it is least equipped to deal effectively with the demands of dialogue because it appears to wash out significant differences between the religions. So a number of Christian theologians, writing from a postmodern, orthodox perspective, have portrayed an approach which claims to respect both orthodoxy and the best expectations of dialogue. Thus, Gavin D'Costa has written that while all thought, including religious thought, cannot avoid its location within a specific tradition, that does not mean that it is closed *to* relationships with other traditions. Basing his approach on orthodox trinitarian theology, especially in respect of the possibility for understanding the power of the Spirit at work beyond the confines of the church, he writes that: 'this trinitarian orientation more rigorously meets the demands for openness, tolerance, and equality that pluralists have stipulated for inter-religious meetings, but in a manner in which all three terms are transformed'.[29] D'Costa's view is not that the Spirit validates other religions as 'structures of salvation' as such, for Christian theology as a tradition-specific enterprise has no warrant for making this judgement. Salvation is not only internal Christian language but also the conciliar Catholic tradition does not lend itself to interpreting other religions in this fashion. What the developing tradition does allow nevertheless is the presence of the Spirit in other cultural traditions, working for the inspiration of the peoples who live within them. From an examination of some central Vatican II and post-conciliar statements D'Costa concludes: 'Hence, it is clear and unambiguous that through the Spirit, God's trinitarian presence within other religions and cultures is a possibility, and one that is discerned by signs of the kingdom inchoately present within that culture.'[30]

There is a tight logic within D'Costa's position. The dangers in seeking an overarching theory which encompasses all religions are many. Yet equally, the question arises whether such a tight logic is sustainable in the face of experience and the pressures of dialogue. In D'Costa's scheme, dialogue and new relationships are not allowed to burst the bounds of orthodoxy's assumptions. Dialogue may reshape 'tradition' but not radically alter its fundamental trajectory. Yet 'tradition' is itself an idealized term, such that Christian history may just as easily be imagined as a process of 'inventiveness', a series of responses to many radically different cultural and historical influences.[31] In other words, there is a myth of stable tradition also.[32] Perhaps a 'looser' understanding of 'tradition' may be more helpful at this stage in the historical development of relations between religions.

But what of D'Costa's use of trinitarian language, especially his concentration on the language of the Spirit? On the promising side, for the purposes of dialogue, is D'Costa's view that the Spirit inspires Christ-like virtues outside of the church, challenges the church to expand its own horizons, reshapes the church in new cultural forms, and judges the church when it has succumbed to anti-Christian powers. As all of this may result from encountering the presence of the Spirit within the religious other, it therefore presents profound reasons for the church to develop dialogical relationships with people of other traditions. But the Spirit does not, as it were, 'roam free'. D'Costa's 'tradition-specific' stance entails finally that 'it is clear that the Spirit cannot be dissociated from Christ'.[33] It is this link which returns the whole discussion to the christological problem.

With this return, D'Costa comes close to repeating his former inclusivist views, whereby other traditions are valid as contexts of the work of the Spirit but ultimately subordinate to the Christian experience of Christ. This is also reflected in his language above that through the Spirit other traditions exhibit an inchoate sense of the kingdom of God which, presumably by comparison, is more fully realized in (Catholic) Christianity.

A major part of the problem with the 'tradition-specific' approach is that one is left with the impression that dialogue exists to serve the ecclesial community and that this is simply a function of the limitations of language under the guidance of postmodern rationality. (Other communities will similarly operate under the limitations of language.) But to go down this route seems too narrow a journey to match the scale of the problem. For it refuses to face squarely the problematic issue of the superiority of Christ and Christianity in relation to the many religions. A great part of the 'tradition-specificity' of Christian history has been the denigration of other faith-traditions.

Tradition-specific theologians are usually unwilling to specu-late about the place of other traditions in the Christian view of history. When they do, however, the argument is rather unconvincing. J. A. DiNoia, for example, opts for what he calls the 'providential diversity of religions':

> other religions are to be valued by Christians, not because they are channels of grace or means of salvation for their adherents, but because they play a real but as yet perhaps not fully specifiable role in the divine plan to which the Christian community bears witness.[34]

This is close to D'Costa's judgement that Christian faith promotes the choate (even if not always realized) sense of the kingdom of God while other faith-traditions have an inkling of the same kingdom yet in an inchoate fashion. For DiNoia this providential role is what he terms 'prospective', by which he means that 'non-Christians will have the opportunity to acknowledge Christ in the future'.[35] This future, for DiNoia, is largely eschatological: in a post-mortem setting, non-Christians will be challenged to embrace the clearer truth of the Christian understanding of our human destiny in the kingdom of God.

I have already responded to this argument in Chapter 3 (p. 46), where it was discussed in terms of the notion of fulfilment. One could add here that this shift towards eschatology is likely to precipitate further dismay from members of other faith-communities. Post-mortem confrontation simply masks the real dilemma that many dialogue partners feel, that is, that they are not really taken seriously as partners in a relationship of parity after all. Rabbi Professor Dan Cohn-Sherbok has reacted to a similar position taken up in the Anglican report, *The Mystery of Salvation*, when he protests: 'What is the point of multifaith dialogue if Christ is the only way to God?'[36]

This chapter began by noting the risk attached to the dialogical enterprise as a whole. The risk was acknowledged above (see p. 105) in the question asked by the Vatican's International Theological Commission. Orthodox theologians committed to dialogical relationships seek to square the circle valiantly, and many examples could be given. But at the end of the day they retain the separation between the twin tracks – one for maintaining the uniqueness of Christ and the other for commitment to dialogue.

The problem is that this entails that the Christian theology of religions experiments with ever diminishing returns and convolutions. For example, when Joseph O'Leary believes that other religious traditions represent 'particular realizations of a universal process, which has become pre-eminently concrete in Jesus Christ',[37] one has surely to ask whether or not the theology has properly caught up with all that the dialogical endeavour is producing. Or when Jacques Dupuis argues for transcending the traditional fulfilment view in favour of the 'mutual complementarity' between Christianity and other traditions, thus leading to 'mutual enrichment' through dialogue, but then avers that 'An eschatological "reheading" (*anakephalaiòsis*) in Christ of the religious traditions will also attain its goal in the fullness of the Reign of God',[38] one cannot but be astonished at the U-turn he has taken.

The pertinent question in the dialogue loop is whether the retention of Christian supremacy undermines the commitment to mutuality, parity and complementarity which dialogue itself assumes, promotes and develops. By various routes I have tried to show how the pluralist option in the theology of religions presents the best prospect for fruitfulness in dialogue. However, there is a warning from critics that ought to be heeded. That is, if letting go of absoluteness is necessary for genuine dialogue this must not be at the cost of dismissing forthright views. Pluralism, however, does not advocate that 'anything goes'; theological and philosophical disagreements are bound to remain.[39]

Notes

1 David Tracy, *Dialogue with the Other: The Inter-Religious Dialogue*, Louvain: Peeters Press and Grand Rapids: Eerdmans 1990, p. 95; cf. the remark by Rita Gross, 'One cannot understand the specificity and uniqueness of one's religion if one does not have a basis for comparison', 'Religious Pluralism: Some Implications for Judaism', *Journal of Ecumenical Studies* 26, no. 1, Winter 1980, p. 41.

2 For example, Keith Ward, *Religion and Revelation* (1994), *Religion and Creation* (1996), *Religion and Human Nature* (1998), *Religion and Community* (2000), all published by Oxford: Clarendon Press; Ninian Smart and Steven Konstantine, *Christian Systematic Theology*, London: HarperCollins, Marshall Pickering 1991; Hans Küng, *Global Responsibility*, London: SCM Press 1991.

3 International Theological Commission, *Christianity and the World Religions*, Vatican 1997, p. 15.

4 This point seems to have been missed by Peter Byrne who argues that 'It is possible to debate the cogency of pluralism, while having no interest in inter-faith dialogue', *Prolegomena to Religious Pluralism: Reference and Realism in Religion*, Basingstoke: Macmillan Press and New York: St Martin's Press 1995, p. 16.

5 Reproduced in James A. Scherer and Stephen B. Bevans (eds), *New Directions in Mission and Evangelization 1, Basic Statements 1974–1991*, chapter 14.

6 Byron L. Sherwin and Harold Kasimow (eds), *John Paul II and Interreligious Dialogue*, Maryknoll: Orbis Press 1999, p. 217.

7 *Redemptoris Missio* 56.

8 'Dialogue and Proclamation', *New Directions*, p. 186.

9 'Dialogue and Proclamation', *New Directions*, p. 184.

10 'Dialogue and Proclamation', *New Directions*, p. 186.

11 '*Redemptoris Missio*', in *New Directions*, p. 176. A more draconian version of this view was voiced through *Dominus Iesus*, the document

issued in 2000 by the Congregation for the Doctrine of the Faith: 'objectively speaking, they [the followers of other religions] are in a gravely deficient situation [22].' The later papal Apostolic Letter, *Novo Millennio Ineunte*, issued in January 2001 to mark the end of the Jubilee Year, reiterated the usual Catholic view: 'It is the primary task of the *missio ad gentes* to announce that it is in Christ, "the Way, and the Truth, and the Life" (Jn 14.6), that people find salvation. Interreligious dialogue "cannot simply replace proclamation, but remains oriented towards proclamation".

12 Sherwin and Kasimow, *John Paul II and Interreligious Dialogue*, p. 217.

13 David Gordis, 'John Paul II and the Jews', *John Paul II and Interreligious Dialogue*, p. 131.

14 For example the WCC World Conference on Mission and Evangelism in 1989, 'Mission in Christ's Way: Your Will Be Done', combined the following two statements: 'In dialogue we are invited to listen in openness to the possibility that the God we know in Jesus Christ may encounter us also in the lives of our neighbours of other faiths . . .' and 'In affirming the dialogical nature of our witness, we are constrained by grace to affirm that "salvation is offered to the whole creation through Jesus Christ"', *New Directions*, pp. 177–200.

15 Paul F. Knitter, 'Between a Rock and a Hard Place: Pluralistic Theology Faces the Ecclesial and Academic Communities', *Journal of Theology*, Summer 1997, p. 80.

16 Knitter, 'Between a Rock and a Hard Place, p. 80.

17 Wilfred Cantwell Smith, 'Shall the Next Century be Secular or Religious?', *Modern Cultures from a Comparative Perspective*, ed. John W. Burbidge, New York: SUNY 1997, p. 81.

18 Eric O. Springsted, 'Conditions of Dialogue: John Hick and Simone Weil', *Journal of Religion* 72, no. 1, January 1992, pp. 22f.

19 Kenneth Surin, for example, has made a career of arguing this way. See his 'Towards a "Materialist" Critique of "Religious Pluralism": A Polemical Examination of the Discourse of John Hick and Wilfred Cantwell Smith', *Religious Pluralism and Unbelief: Studies Critical and Comparative*, ed. Ian Hamnet, London and New York: Routledge 1990, chapter 8. Also see the essays by Lesslie Newbigin, Jürgen Moltmann, John Milbank, and Kenneth Surin, in Gavin D'Costa (ed.), *Christian Uniqueness Reconsidered: The Myth of a Pluralistic Theology of Religions*, Maryknoll: Orbis Press 1990.

20 For example, see the forthright book, Paul Knitter, *One Earth, Many Religions: Multifaith Dialogue and Global Responsibility*, Maryknoll: Orbis Books 1995.

21 Gavin D'Costa, *The Meeting of Religions and the Trinity*, Edinburgh: T&T Clark and Maryknoll: Orbis Books 2000, p. 26.

22 D'Costa, *The Meeting of Religions and the Trinity*, p. 30.

23 John Hick, *The Rainbow of Faiths: Critical Dialogues on Religious Pluralism*, London: SCM Press 1995, p. 50.

24 J. A. DiNoia, *The Diversity of Religions*, The Catholic University of America Press 1992, p. 63.

25 *World Scripture: A Comparative Anthology of Sacred Texts*, ed. Andrew Wilson, New York: Paragon House 1995.

26 Maurice Wiles, however, has made use of an analogy developed by Richard Miller, which tells how different hunters may track an animal using different methods and wisdoms from their social histories, and yet be tracking the same animal – leading to the view that a significant overlap in the descriptions of the animal need not be a criterion for knowing that they are all tracking the same animal. See his *Christian Theology and Inter-Religious Dialogue*, London: SCM Press 1992, pp. 39f.

27 Sumner B. Twiss, 'The Philosophy of Religious Pluralism: A Critical Appraisal of Hick and His Critics', *The Journal of Religion* 70, no. 4, October 1990, p. 567, italics mine.

28 Twiss, 'The Philosophy of Religious Pluralism', p. 544.

29 D'Costa, *The Meeting of Religions and the Trinity*, p. 99.

30 D'Costa, *The Meeting of Religions and the Trinity*, p. 114

31 See my 'Christianity: 2000 Years of Inventiveness', *Encounters: Journal of Inter-Cultural Perspectives* 6, no. 1, March 2000, pp. 3–24.

32 Cf. Robert Wilken, *The Myth of Christian Beginnings*, London: SCM Press 1979.

33 D'Costa, *The Meeting of Religions and the Trinity*, p. 110.

34 DiNoia, *The Diversity of Religions*, p. 91.

35 DiNoia, *The Diversity of Religions*, p. 107.

36 Dan Cohn-Sherbok, 'Strait is the Gate, and I Shan't Get Through', *Church Times*, 26 January 1996, p. 8.

37 Cited by Jacques Dupuis, SJ, *Toward a Christian Theology of Religious Pluralism*, Maryknoll: Orbis Press 1997.

38 Dupuis, *Toward a Christian Theology of Religious Pluralism*, p. 389.

39 John Hick discusses disagreement between religions at three levels: historical, metaphysical and imaging Ultimate Reality. See *An Interpretation of Religion: Human Responses to the Transcendent*, London: Macmillan Press 1989, chapter 20.

7

Prospects for a Global Ethic?

At the heart of the basic vision of Christian faith and of all post-axial religions is the summons to transcend the narrow interests that confine our belonging to ethnic groups, tribes, local cultures or nations. In ethical terms, the vision embraces the virtues that do not specifically privilege the group in which they have taken root. These include, in varying degrees and according to the emphases of specific religious insights, at least the following: compassion towards others, social justice, inclusion of strangers, peace, unity of all peoples, care of the natural world. Yet history teaches us that obedience to this summons has proved highly elusive.

Failure to follow through the basic ethical vision in practice has proved especially applicable in relations between the religions. The report prepared by the Millennium Institute for the third Parliament of the World's Religions (1999) expressed alarm at this state of affairs when the global context is emphasized: 'the greatest single scandal in which Earth's faith traditions are now involved is their failure to practise their highest ethical ideals in their relations with one another.'[1] In addition to historical and political factors, rivalry between religions, suspicions of the other, and fear of differences have cumulatively undermined any moves towards interreligious co-operation and dialogue, the potential and imperative for which lies in basic religious vision itself.

The paradox at the ethical level, in a dialogical context, is that while the values of universal compassion, justice, peace, and so on, point in the direction of the religions co-operating for the greater good, their absolutist belief structures, cultural constructions and memories of violent antagonisms propel them apart. This chapter explores the hypothesis of a Global Ethic as a significant proposal for negotiating this paradox as a dialogue of basic ethical values.

Beginning with the World

Perhaps the main reason why global ethic thinking is potentially attractive is simply the pragmatic one that the world desperately needs it. The problems facing the human race on a global scale are well known: escalating ecological degradation allied to over-population and overconsumption; geo-political disorientation and international realignments since the ending of the Cold War; continuing after-effects of western colonialism; deepening economic inequalities between the developed and the developing nations, and between rich and poor in both developed and the developing nations; entrenched militarism together with the threats that arise from the arms trade and the manufacture of weapons of mass destruction, including the new generation of sophisticated 'missile defence systems'; HIV/AIDS and other epidemics which show no sign of abating. Sadly, any list could be extended, along with feelings of impending gloom. Those who paint an apocalyptic picture of the future can do so with good reasons.

Yet apocalyptic scenarios are not necessarily self-fulfilling. Part of the stimulus they provide is to alert us to potential dangers and terrors, rather than to push us further into pessimism. In an age that has learned the extent of human responsibility in freedom, this function is vital. Therefore, the need to tackle our global problems seems sufficient reason alone for the religions, with their visions of ethical transformation for the good, to suspend their ancient antagonisms and learn co-operation.[2]

It is clear that a well-grounded ethical response to the crises facing the global future requires more than a strategy of pragmatic collaboration, if the hiatus between ethical theory and practice is to be overcome. Discussing the role of comparative religious ethics in the face of global crises, Bruce Grelle pushes beyond the pragmatic response and draws attention to the underlying issue of the balance between unity and diversity that is required:

Many contemporary issues require an international response, and a sympathetic awareness of diverse worldviews and values is a first step toward building the understanding, cooperation, and larger 'sense of the whole' that will be required in order to address many of the global issues . . . in the next several decades.[3]

That said, it seems obvious that the Christian or any other tradition alone does not have the resources to meet the new challenges. Therefore we need to ask what shape our dialogical co-operation with other worldviews and religions might take for this new ethical endeavour to succeed.

A Global Ethic

One suggestion which has received considerable attention in recent years as a possible starting-point for a dialogical inter-religious approach to the 'larger "sense of the whole"' centres on the notion of a Global Ethic. There are in fact two main texts associated with a Global Ethic in circulation to date. One is the more well-known text prepared by Hans Küng and adopted as *Towards a Global Ethic: An Initial Declaration* at the second Parliament of the World's Religions, held in Chicago in 1993. The other was devised by Leonard Swidler, as 'A Universal Declaration of a Global Ethic'. Both Declarations can be found in Swidler's edited book *For All Life: Toward a Universal Declaration of a Global Ethic*.[4] Apart from some differences in style and emphasis, both versions share an overall agreement, and represent the fruit of dialogue over many years. For simplicity of reference, I shall concentrate on the text adopted at the second Parliament of the World's Religions, but involve responses to both drafts as part of my discussion.

As a first comment on the shape of the Global Ethic, it is worth noting its analogous structural resemblance to my *Cycle of Religious Life* (see Chapter 1). Setting this out in diagrammatic form will also help to underline the four main principles governing a Global Ethic:

Diagnostic Principle 1
No new global order without a new global ethic

Goal Principle 4
A Transformation
of Consciousness

Revelatory Principle 2
Fundamental demand:
Every human being must
be treated humanely

Recommended Practice Principle 3
Four Irrevocable Directives:

(a) Commitment to a culture of non-violence and respect for life
(b) Commitment to a culture of solidarity and a just economic order
(c) Commitment to a culture of tolerance and a life of truthfulness
(d) Commitment to a culture of equal rights and partnership between men and women

A Global Ethic by definition caters for many ethical perspectives and must be the fruits of more than interreligious conversation alone. Therefore, humanist and secularist, as well as religious, perspectives are invited to share the movement depicted by the four principles, all of which are humanity-based. However, presenting a Global Ethic in this diagrammatic form clarifies the religious inspiration behind it. This allows those whose ethical outlook is shaped by their religious commitments to enter a Global Ethic knowing that it reflects their interests.

The following initial comments on the cycle can now be made:

Diagnostic Principle 1: states that the many global threats confronting humankind require a response not only at a practical level but also at a level that reflects fundamental values. It judges that there is need for a new global ethic in response to changing world circumstances and in line with an increasingly positive appreciation of ethical plurality, including religious plurality. Without such an ethic the prospects for economic, political, social and ecological stability are precarious. Global stability requires consensus at more than simply political or legal levels of agreement, for a well-grounded ethical vision rests on 'hopes, goals, ideals, standards'. Moreover, faith-communities bear a particular burden: 'it is the communities of faith who bear a responsibility to demonstrate that such hopes, ideals, and standards can be guarded, grounded and lived'.⁵

Revelatory Principle 2: corresponds, on the ethical level, to the imaginative disclosure of transcendent meaning. Here the framers of a Global Ethic observed that all religions harbour a version of the so-called Golden Rule: 'There is a principle which is found and has persisted in many religious and ethical traditions of humankind for thousands of years: *What you do not wish done to yourself, do not do to others.* Or, in positive terms: *What you wish done to yourself, do to others!* This should be the irrevocable, unconditional norm for all areas of life, for families and communities, for races, nations, and religions.'⁶ In one sense the Golden Rule is of such generality as to be of little consequence. However, its virtue is that it opens the door to the prospects of possible cross-cultural and cross-religious criteria for judging basic moral values.

Recommended Practice Principle 3: begins to flesh out the direction for the application of the Golden Rule. The *'four broad, ancient guidelines* for human behaviour which are found in most of the religions of the world' correspond to a religio-ethical pathway of recovery in response to the disclosure of transcendent meaning within the religions.⁷ They provide the bridge between the religious basis for ethical life and its practical outworking. Again, although they are couched in generalized language – who could be *against* these kinds of commitment? – they express what has not always been taken for granted in the religions. In this way, the four Directives contain the seeds for radicalizing ethical demands at the concrete level.

Goal Principle 4: envisages the goal of ethical life as transformation: 'Earth cannot be changed for the better unless we achieve a transformation in the consciousness of individuals and in public life.'⁸ Not only does the religious response to global threats require sound analysis based on multidisciplinary scientific principles in the spheres of politics, economics and so on, it also demands a change of heart in individuals and in public life. The adoption of a Global Ethic, while attempting to reflect ancient guidelines, nevertheless challenges the representatives of the world's ethical systems to develop their own ethical formulations in dialogue with other worldviews and in relation to the changing needs of the global future.

There are practical and theoretical problems associated with the very notion – some might say pretentiousness – of a Global Ethic. The practical concerns centre on its status: who 'owns' it and what would it mean for a Global Ethic to achieve global acceptance? These seem to me to be largely problems of representation and participation in the developments of intercultural and interreligious life through the dialogical process. Calls have been made to extend not only the discussion of an existing Global Ethic but also to widen the franchise on the production of such an ethic. As Leonard Swidler appeals: 'A Global Ethic must work on all three levels: scholars, leaders, grassroots', as well as across traditions.[9] That is to say, different religious representatives from within different streams of global religious life should add to the production of a Global Ethic from their own particular cultural and religious perspectives. These would not be, say, a Buddhist or Islamic or Christian Global Ethic, but a Global Ethic written from particular standpoints yet embracing what could be considered to be a consensus on shared values across traditions.

Serious theoretical questions arise with a Global Ethic. Can a Global Ethic be other than an homogenizing of religious differences and so turn out unwittingly to be dismissive of the richness of global diversity itself? Does the Declaration conceal a normative thrust in addition to its claim to embody a moderate consensus on shared values? Matters of both desirability and feasibility are being raised here, and I shall discuss each area in turn.

Desirable?

Is a Global Ethic desirable? At least two closely related issues are clustered within this question. The first is: in a plural world, why should *this* type of project be the only or even the best foundation for religious ethics in a globally shared world? The world is threatened, certainly, and in an interconnected world threats are not in slavery to boundaries, be they geographical, cultural or religious. But is a Global Ethic in fact a covert absolutist form of ethics? In this regard, Sallie King, an American scholar in Religious Studies and Buddhist practitioner, sounds a warning and a question: 'It is indeed an odd expression of modernity to issue an absolutist statement such as the Global Ethic. How can such a thing be justified in the modern world?'[10]

What response to this accusation can be given? Part of a response was given in the full text of the *Initial Declaration* itself:

> By a *global ethic* we do not mean a global ideology or a *single unified religion* beyond all existing religions, and certainly not the domination of one religion over all others. By a global ethic we mean a *fundamental consensus on binding values, irrevocable standards, and personal attitudes*. Without such a fundamental consensus on an ethic, sooner or later every community will be threatened by chaos or dictatorship, and individuals will despair.[11]

As historical change generates both hope and alarm, new possibilities and new threats in culture, it is invariably accompanied by concerns regarding basic values. From a perspective that celebrates plural responses, a positive ethic based on shared values need not fear the charge of absolutism, for it leaves room for differences of interpretation according to the diversity of the globe's cultural and religious life.

Precisely how a 'fundamental consensus' might be able to combine with differences of interpretation within wider ethical frameworks has been suggested by the Princeton social scientist, Michael Walzer, in his distinction between 'thin' and 'thick' morality.[12] 'Thin' morality (or 'minimal morality') refers to 'a whole set of elementary ethical standards, which include the fundamental right to life, to just treatment (also from the state), to physical and mental integrity'.[13] There are universal values that arise, almost intuitively, when human beings are faced with oppression or unfair treatment. Such values are limited to fundamental demands such as truth and justice, and are capable of being harnessed as '*a certain kind of universalism*'.[14] 'Thick' morality, on the other hand, indicates the differentiated morality of particular peoples and cultures, where interpretations of fundamental norms and principles may vary widely according to cultural history, religious commitment, and other social and political factors. They may also in some respects be in definite contrast or even opposition. But the wide variations need not necessarily undermine any orientation on fundamental values. These values are not abstractly constructed, as with Enlightenment theories of justice and value, but spring from concrete situations, and therefore can potentially claim a wide allegiance.

Sallie King herself acknowledges the value of some universalizing of perspective, notably in the area of human rights: 'People all over the world recognize that if they don't want their own basic human rights violated, their best bet is to try to prevent all human rights violations. Hence, the nearly universal acceptance of the principles and languages of human rights.'[15] In which case, why should a Global Ethic be outlawed as undesirable, especially when it seeks no more than a minimal agreement on 'binding values, irrevocable standards, and personal attitudes'?

A second objection to the desirability of a Global Ethic stems from what some perceive as its intrinsic linkage with the internationalizing/globalizing of one particular (western) culture, or at least its tacit approval of western culture by avoiding any strong critique of the effects of such internationalization/globalization. The complaint is that the generalized statements of a 'thin' morality or a 'fundamental consensus' housed in a Global Ethic do nothing to alter the desperate plight of the world's (increasing) poor. Indeed, they might make that plight worse by being open to manipulation by the economically and politically powerful.

There is some justification in these complaints, for if global ethic thinking does not offer at least a starting-point for dealing with factors such as the unequal distribution of wealth in the world then it had better be abandoned. But the complaints should be interpreted as sounding a warning rather than as calling a halt to the project of a Global Ethic as a whole. It is true that the pressure for a Global Ethic occurs at the same historical moment as other 'internationalizing' tendencies, yet surely this does not invalidate its purpose as such?[16] There may be risks that projects like the Global Ethic unintentionally participate in the destructive effects of 'internationalization', but there is nothing inherent in them entailing that they do.

A Global Ethic is not allied to any particular economic, social and political analysis of societies and their internal and external relationships. As a statement of fundamental values it aims to create a broad matrix of dialogical understanding. In the application of global ethics, in specific cultural and religious contexts, the voices of the victims need to be heard again and again, and the destructive excesses of 'economic globalization' exposed. Yet, even at a generalized level, the four 'Irrevocable Directives' point in the direction for transforming systems that create undue suffering and inequality. More specifically, the full text of the Global Ethic makes clear its commitment to economic justice:

> Where power and wealth are accumulated ruthlessly, feelings of envy, resentment, and deadly hatred and rebellion inevitably well up in the disadvantaged and marginalized. This leads to a vicious circle of violence and counter-violence. Let no one be deceived: There is no global peace without global justice![17]

Precisely how global economic justice is to be achieved is a matter of dispute and disagreement, but it is beyond the remit of a Global Ethic to enter the details of this debate, though it is aware that 'conflicts of interest are unavoidable'.

Rising to the challenge of this critique, some theologians of dialogue have argued that global eco-human suffering provides the essential motive and *locus* for ethical dialogue between religions. Most eloquent and forceful among these has been Paul Knitter. Arguing against both the postmodern theologians, who would curtail the communicable potential between religions, and the ecclesial world, which would base all on Christ, Knitter argues: 'If persons from different religious traditions respond *together* to the obligation of doing something about the sufferings that are destroying human and ecological life, they will find themselves *graced* with a new opportunity to understand and communicate and learn from each other.'[18] Knitter calls this an ethic of responsibility in the face of suffering, an ethic which neither requires agreement at conceptual levels prior to dialogue nor goes against the grain of the Christian message, in so far as this message reflects the 'kingdom' values of inclusiveness, justice and compassion.

Knitter's view is not simply a pragmatic one; he is not just talking of the necessity to tackle the world's desperate problems through collaborations across many boundaries, welcome as that most certainly is. For Knitter, interreligious collaboration is itself a form of experiencing the sacred in life:

> Working together for justice becomes or can become, a *communicatio in sacris* – a communication in the Sacred – available to us beyond our churches and temples.

> When we are acting for justice, when we are acting for the sustainability of the environment, we are acting not only with other humans but with a Reality or Process or Truth that sustains our activities.[19]

It is at the point when Knitter moves from interreligious collaboration to this suggestion of 'a communication in the Sacred' that questions arise concerning his view of global ethics in relation to the diversity of religious traditions. Is this something that can be supported by the basic ethical visions of the religions? Or does his referral of everything to eco-human suffering derive from sources outside Christian faith and the other religions?

By proposing eco-human suffering as the reason for interreligious dialogue in the context of global ethic thinking, Knitter has been accused of a new form of absolutism. (This is ironic, as Knitter's proposals are also directed as a cautionary warning to any complacency that may accompany the initial declaration of a Global Ethic offered both by the Parliament of Religions and by Leonard Swidler.)[20] So Gavin D'Costa complains that Knitter's summons to rally round the defence of the 'suffering poor' and the 'suffering earth' as foci for interreligious dialogue and global ethics is not the radical idea it seems to be: 'Knitter unwittingly perpetuates modernity's project in employing unmediated foundational ethical universals, and he is driven to this in trying to find a universal site for interreligious agreement. The problem is that he constructs such a site, rather than naturally finds it.'[21]

D'Costa's critique of Knitter is similar to the one made against Hick (see above, p. 112ff.), that the criteria by which Christian faith and the religions are judged is not some agreed interreligious universal (even if that was possible) but a Kantian 'exclusivist modernity'. Against Knitter, he terms this curiously 'a form of neo-pagan-unitarianism'.[22] Along with their differences in respect of beliefs, the religions construe both suffering and nature differently, thus ruling out the 'common ground' of dialogue envisaged as eco-human suffering. When the point of dialogue is already known – to pursue action for the sake of healing eco-human suffering – then, according to D'Costa, what is the point of dialogue as such?

I have responded to some of the elements of this critique above (p. 113f.). Here it remains to say that there seems to be something opaque about the raw experience of suffering which cannot be constrained by its definitions in religious languages. Of course the traditions do speak of suffering in different terms, but language is not a prison. The problem of cross-cultural and cross-religious communication does not mean that suffering cannot act as a rallying point for dialogue and collaboration across traditions. This is often evident in situations of *extremis*. 'When we talk about the Holocaust,' says John Cobb, 'few dare to say this is a linguistic event which has reality only as it comes to speech ... That raises ethical issues, and we can ask about the different responses to these issues on the part of Christians and Jews.'[23] Some forms of suffering *are – have to be* – shared sites for dialogue.

Further support for the desirability of a Global Ethic, and picking up the theme of suffering in the contexts of human rights discussion, can be found in the following African perspective from Mutombo Nkulu:

> The African continent, more and more neglected by the masters of the world economy while its governments fall apart and Africans suffer starvation and ethnic cleansing, is not in a good situation. This 'lost continent' as some pessimistic scholars call it again, needs such a thing as a Global Ethic that can rescue it from its own diseases and save it through a 'global solidarity.' At the same time its experience of suffering and struggle for survival may be fruitful for other peoples. For suffering is a privileged instance for the understanding of human rights.[24]

'Global solidarity', it would seem, requires a 'Global Ethic'. Nkulu demonstrates how the African Charter of Human and Peoples' Rights has many points of overlap with Swidler's and Küng's declarations of a Global Ethic. This creates the possibility for two-way traffic: the relevance of a Global Ethic for African ethical reflections and the contribution from Africa, especially through its experience of suffering, to the sharpening up of a Global Ethic in support of the marginalized and the 'lost'. There seems no difficulty here in accepting the experience of suffering as the focus for dialogue about a Global Ethic.

Feasible?

Let me turn now to the second layer of objections that have been made against global ethic thinking. Granted that a Global Ethic is desirable, is it feasible? The answer to this depends on whether the tension between universality and religious diversity can be entered into creatively. This has already been implicit in the question of desirability, but now I approach it from another angle.

At one level, support for a Global Ethic has already been proved in so far as the momentum behind the project has been gaining ground for some time. Many academic voices and religious leaders have given backing to it. Introducing his own multiple collection, Küng comments: 'Taken together, all these very different voices witness to the fact that in the matter of a Global Ethic a growing awareness is already developing in many religions and cultures.'[25]

Notwithstanding the enthusiasm for a Global Ethic from many quarters, however, there is widespread suspicion that the theological and philosophical problem of the tension between the universality/absolutism of theological ethics and the historical diversity of ethical histories/cultures requires more rigorous attention than it has so far received.

In order to approach this debate, a useful comparison can again be drawn from the field of human rights. There have been many voices raised against that *Declaration* on the grounds that it is not universal enough, and that it could never fully reflect the competing ethical aspirations of different cultural groups in an overarching framework. However, a useful worldwide study project on 'Religion and Human Rights' has reported that many of the assumptions made concerning the incompatibility between universality and respect for diversity in human rights tend to be exaggerated. As one of the editors of the report, Sumner Twiss, has commented: 'human rights set aspirational norms, and no persuasive case has been made to show that human rights as a goal for all peoples is either illegitimate or unattainable'.[26] This highly suggestive observation could be applied in the case of a Global Ethic. In so far as a Global Ethic seeks a 'fundamental consensus on binding values, irrevocable standards, and personal attitudes' it seeks a comparable aspirational norm and goal. The 'Religion and Human Rights' research further noted a distinction between corrupt leaders and oppressed peoples in the use they made of local and culturally specific traditions. Corrupt leaders used local traditions 'as a smoke screen to deflect attention away from the abuses they perpetrate on their own citizens'; while advocacy groups defending the poor 'use elements of local culture and religion to translate human rights into cultural idioms so that they might be more effectively recognized and respected'. And most importantly: 'the group found that many oppressed peoples – regardless of their cultural locations and differences – have little difficulty accepting the ideas of universal human rights'.[27]

These findings echo the 'thick' and 'thin' distinction noted earlier, between a differentiated and fuller expression of ethical values based on specific traditions and a minimal consensus on fundamental values between traditions. Global ethical values akin to global human rights values could be embraced as binding on all peoples, cultures and traditions; while the scope for the translating/interpreting of these values into more specific terms, thereby safeguarding the diversity of religion and culture, remains wide. The task of balancing the global with the local constitutes the very *raison d'être* of dialogue.[28]

Twiss illustrates the feasibility of a Global Ethic further by demonstrating the compatibility between the language of universal rights and affirmation of rights based on locally specific normative values. First, the UN *Universal Declaration of Human Rights*, while embodying the language of western thought, is the product of actual cross-cultural interaction. It is not a purely western product that is not really applicable to other cultures, as is sometimes alleged. The universality was present, historically, from the beginning and has been strengthened since 1948 by further enactments of human rights that have emphasized socio-economic rights and the collective rights of whole peoples and groups, rights that are often considered to be more 'traditional' or 'eastern' in emphasis. Therefore, the usually perceived 'unbridge-able division' between individual and collective rights is largely a chimera. As Twiss concludes: 'No one tradition is the sole source of human rights values, and these values are not exclu-sively Western'; and that international human rights 'represent a shared vision of moral and social values compatible with a variety of religious and cultural worldviews – a unity within a diversity'.[29]

Further support for this compatibility is elicited by Twiss – in a second move of his argument – that demonstrates how Confucian and Indigenous traditions, which are usually consid-ered to be hostile to human rights (at least in their supposed dominance by individualistic concerns), are able to support human rights so long as the necessity for balance between indivi-dual and communal rights is respected. Moreover, once we recognize that human rights are also an evolving matter, these traditions are poised to make their own contributions to a continuing human rights story.

The implications for global ethic thinking of the relationships between universal human rights and culturally determined rights are manifold. The universal values are not an abstraction nor a product of one culture alone, though they were initiated as a result of one culture's (the European) experiences of genocide and devastation in two world wars. But they do represent a set of values that are both shared and yet malleable in respect of their openness to interpretation by a diverse range of cultural and religious perspectives. Moreover, a dialogical relationship between specific cultures contributes towards the evolution of universal values, maintaining the balance between universality and specific interpretations. Religious frameworks will both be challenged by the universal thrust of agreed fundamental values and make their own contribution to a continuing enterprise. 'Thick' and 'thin', 'particular' and 'universal' balances match the feasibility of a Global Ethic that is 'maximal in intended scope' and 'minimal in normative content'.

Additional support for the evidence submitted by Twiss (and the application by me of its potential in the discussions of a Global Ethic) stems from a study of the reception of human rights in relation to the major world religions. Following a substantial survey of the shifts towards the affirmation of human rights and its advocacy among the religions, Robert Traer concludes: 'The different theories of human rights may not suggest a global faith, but the practice of human rights advocacy does.'[30] This is in complete alignment with the work of the Religion and Human Rights group and its interpretation by Twiss. Bridging the discourses of human rights and religious affiliation, Traer further adds: 'From the evidence presented, one can conclude that faith in human rights reflects a convergence of the religious wisdom of the world.'[31] Should we not say that if this has been the achievement in the arena of human rights, could the same not be possible in the arena of a Global Ethic?

Dialogical Future

If a Global Ethic is both desirable and feasible this is not to say that it is without problems. Negotiating the alleged incommensurability of religious traditions with a common reference point has obvious theoretical difficulties. Yet a start has been made. Support from diverse religious traditions, including the Christian, can be elaborated. Dialogue between traditions is destined to strengthen its potential as an agreement on (minimum) fundamental values that are interpreted variously from particular and specific (maximum) perspectives.

Some might still imagine that any declaration of 'minimum ethics' is bound to seem anodyne. Between 'thick' and 'thin' ethics, it is the 'thick' that provides more bite. However, it would be wrong to assume that a Global Ethic is so thin as to be simply transparent. The four Irrevocable Directives themselves provide for a substantial critique of the destructive effects of human behaviour. 'Commitment to respect for all life' is the basis for a critique of policies that fail to support environmental sustainability or continue militarization of international relations.

'Commitment to a just economic order' intrinsically raises doubts about the long-term benefits of unbridled Capitalism. 'Commitment to a life of tolerance and truthfulness' promotes human respect and celebrates the differences between histories and cultures. 'Commitment to partnership between men and women' is a goal that most religions and cultures have yet to honour.

It is in the details ('thick' ethics) that the struggle to embody these commitments will be most keenly felt. Moreover, it is true that there is a considerable tension at the heart of a Global Ethic, as it strives to be both a consensus on *'those things which we already hold in common now'* and a challenge to be realized in the face of the many threats to the future of the planet. How this tension is 'resolved' is a challenge in itself. Keith Ward has written how the tensions can be approached:

> It might be better to see the different faiths, not as in radical opposition but as having a range of agreed values, but varying ways of interpreting them in the light of a developing understanding of the world. There is an important sense in which differing faiths are engaged in a common pursuit of supreme value, though they conceive this in diverse ways.[32]

The reference to the 'common pursuit of supreme value' raises again all the issues of incommensurability between the traditions and their possible common ground. Ward's own view is that these are best tackled on the pluralist-like model of 'convergence'.[33] For myself, I am persuaded of the more full-blooded pluralist case as the best option for achieving what seems to be needed – the reinterpretation of absoluteness in religious commitment that creates the theological/philosophical conditions fully for different voices to be heard under the conditions of 'rough parity'.

But Ward's point about a 'developing understanding of the world' is well made. The Global Ethic process has been enhanced in recent years by the extension of its central concerns into more practical areas. These can be seen particularly in the InterAction Council's *A Universal Declaration of Human Responsibilities*,[34] the *Earth Charter*,[35] and the *Call to Our Guiding Institutions* from the Council for a Parliament of the World's Religions.[36] The latter seeks to integrate global ethical values into the major spheres of institutional influence around the world – specified by the Parliament as 'Government', 'Agriculture, Labour and Commerce', 'Religion and Spirituality', 'Science and Medicine', 'Education', 'Arts and Communications Media', 'International Intergovernmental Organizations', and 'Organizations of Civil Society'. The value of a humanity-based Global Ethic, as opposed to normative religiously based ethics, lies in its potential for being absorbed by the powers and forces that shape the world. In this way it can act as a 'broker' between the differently construed religious ethics of the religions and the world of practical choice.

However, a Global Ethic will only be able to achieve this role if it is presented as a non-absolute framework. If a Global Ethic forms the basis of a call to our guiding institutions then it must include humility as part of its invitation. As a largely dialogically driven process, the humility is built in to its intentions (even if humility is not always apparent). But as a process driven also by ethical interests grounded in a sense of transcendence, global ethics thinking exists on the knife-edge between offering the world the wisdom of its own religious treasures (dialogically orientated) and being open to receive new wisdom from the institutionalized world of hard choices. This can be construed as a tension between respect both for democratic liberal openness and for traditional cultures and religions. It has been described well by Steven Rockefeller, as follows:

> The democratic way means respect for and openness to all cultures, but it also challenges all cultures to abandon those intellectual and moral values that are inconsistent with the ideals of freedom, equality and the on-going co-operative experimental search for truth and well-being. It is a creative method of transformation.[37]

There is a price to be paid for signing up with a Global Ethic!

Yet even the liberal ideals of democratic openness and freedom are prone to absolutism. It is in fact one of the criticisms of postmodernism that the era of liberal absoluteness has now come to an end, and that the impact of plurality is partly the cause of this demise. However, there are reasons for thinking that a retreat into different religious corners, where the absoluteness of tradition retains at least the appearance of remaining in tact, is both practically disastrous and theoretically untenable. A pluralistic and dialogical future remains as the option best suited to a global future.

It is an essential part of global ethic thinking that the function of dialogue is to mediate between agreements on fundamental values and the larger ethical pictures preserved severally by the various faith-stances, religious and secular. As it does so it will encourage the laying down of absolutisms of whatever shape. Therefore we shall all be changed in the process. This is the real potential of the project called Global Ethic.

Notes

1 Gerald O. Barney, with contributors, *Threshold 2000: Critical Issues and Spiritual Values for a Global Age*, Michigan: CoNexus Press, Millennium Institute 1999, p. 108.

2 See the collection, *True to This Earth: Global Challenges and Transforming Faith*, ed. Alan Race and Roger Williamson, Oxford: Oneworld Publications 1995, for an analysis of global issues and theological responses across a range of issues.

3 Bruce Grelle, 'Scholarship and Citizenship: Comparative Religious Ethicists as Public Intellectuals', *Explorations in Global Ethics: Comparative Religious Ethics and Interreligious Dialogue*, ed. Sumner B. Twiss and Bruce Grelle, Boulder, Colorado and Oxford: Westview Press 1998, p. 45.

4 Published by White Cloud Press, Oregon 1998.

5 Hans Küng and Karl-Josef Kuschel (eds), *A Global Ethic: The Declaration of the Parliament of the World's Religions*, London: SCM Press 1993, p. 20; and Leonard Swidler (ed.), *For All Life: Toward a Universal Declaration of a Global Ethic*, Oregon: White Cloud Press 1998, p. 41.

6 *A Global Ethic*, pp. 23f., and *For All Life*, p. 43.

7 *A Global Ethic*, p. 24, and *For All Life*, p. 44.

8 *A Global Ethic*, p. 34, and *For All Life*, p. 50.

9 *For All Life*, p. 25; cf. Peggy Morgan and Marcus Braybrooke (eds), *Testing the Global Ethic: Voices from Religious Traditions on Moral Values*, Oxford: International Interfaith Centre and World Congress of Faiths, and Michigan: CoNexus Press 1998. *For All Life* contains many responses from different traditions on the prospects for a Global Ethic,

some commenting on Swidler's draft and some calling for the production of a Global Ethic from specific religious perspectives.

10 *Explorations in Global Ethics*, p. 125.

11 *A Global Ethic*, p. 21, and *For All Life*, p. 42; cf. Swidler's own statement in *For All Life*, p. 30: 'Furthermore, none of our traditions, ethical or religious, is satisfied with minimums, vital as they are; rather, because humans are endlessly self-transcending, our traditions also provide maximums to be striven for. Consequently, this declaration does the same.'

12 Michael Walzer, *Thick and Thin: Moral Argument at Home and Abroad*, Indiana: Notre Dame Press 1994.

13 Hans Küng, *A Global Ethic for Global Politics and Economics*, London: SCM Press 1997, p. 95.

14 Cited by Küng, *A Global Ethic for Global Politics and Economics*, p. 97.

15 Sallie King, 'A Global Ethic in the Light of Comparative Religious Ethics,' *Explorations in Global Ethics*, p. 137.

16 John Hick has called this tie-up between two types of response to the pressures of globalization 'guilt by association'. He writes, in *The Rainbow of Faiths: Critical Dialogues on Religious Pluralism*, London: SCM Press 1995, p. 39: 'Contemporary religious pluralism is part of the same world as multinational captalism; but surely it doesn't follow that religious pluralism is an ally of international capitalism and its repressive universalizing effects.' Though Hick was not making this point in the context of global ethics discussion, it is relevant for these discussions also. Published also as *A Christian Theology of Religions*, Louisville: Westminster/John Knox Press 1995.

17 *A Global Ethic*, pp. 27f., and *For All Life*, p. 46.

18 Paul F. Knitter, 'Between a Rock and a Hard Place: Pluralistic Theology Faces the Ecclesial and Academic Communities', *Journal of Theology*, Summer 1997, p. 92. See the fuller treatment of this position in his *One Earth, Many Religions: Multifaith Dialogue and Global Responsibility*, Maryknoll: Orbis Press 1995.

19 Knitter, *One Earth, Many Religions*, pp. 112–17.

20 Knitter is highly critical about a Global Ethic which is not alert to its own ideological colouring, in his article 'Pitfalls and Promises for a Global Ethic', *Buddhist-Christian Studies* 15, 1995. But in his *One Earth, Many Religions*, p. 72, after entering caveats and reservations, he is able to endorse it: 'Küng's proposal, though it may be much more complex than he realizes, and though it will have to be pursued more cautiously and in different forms than he suggests, is one which , I believe, an ever greater number of persons and nations throughout the world can endorse.'

21 Gavin D'Costa, *The Meeting of Religions and the Trinity*, Edinburgh: T&T Clark 2000, p. 34.

22 D'Costa, *The Meeting of Religions and the Trinity*, p. 39.

23 John B. Cobb, Jr, 'Can Comparative Religious Ethics Help?', *Transforming Christianity and the World: A Way Beyond Absolutism and Relativism*, edited and introduced by Paul Knitter, Maryknoll: Orbis Books 1999, p. 162.

24 Mutombo Nkulu, 'The African Charter on Human Rights: An African Contribution to the Global Ethic Project', *For All Life*, p. 94.

25 Cf. Hans Küng, *Yes to a Global Ethic*, London: SCM Press 1996, and Swidler, *For All Life*.

26 Sumner B. Twiss, 'Religion and Human Rights: A Comparative Perspective', *Explorations in Global Ethics*, p. 158. See also the original project report: John Kelsay and Sumner B. Twiss (eds), *Religion and Human Rights*, published by The Project on Religion and Human Rights, New York 1994.

27 Twiss, 'Religion and Human Rights', p. 158.

28 Of the two Global Ethic statements in existence the Middle Principles of the one by Leonard Swidler is modelled most closely on the UN *Universal Declaration of Human Rights*. See also Swidler's *Religious Liberty and Human Rights in Nations and Religions*, New York: Hippocrene & Ecumenical Press 1986; and *Theoria to Praxis: How Jews, Chrisians, and Muslims Can Together Move from Theory to Practice*, Leuven: Peeters 1998.

29 Twiss, 'Religion and Human Rights', pp. 161f.

30 Robert Traer, *Faith in Human Rights*, Washington: Georgetown University Press 1991, pp. 207f.

31 Traer, *Faith in Human Rights*, p. 219.

32 Keith Ward, *A Vision to Pursue: Beyond the Crisis in Christianity*, London: SCM Press 1991, p. 190.

33 See his impressive studies leaning towards 'convergence', all published by Clarendon Press, Oxford: *Religion and Revelation: A Theology of Revelation in the World's Religions*, 1994; *Religion and Creation*, 1996; *Religion and Human Nature*, 1998; *Religion and Community*, 2000. I discuss Ward's views further in Chapter 8. See also John Hick's defence of Pluralism against Ward's criticisms on the grounds that Ward retains a personalist view of the Ultimate, and this is a view which cannot cater for the values inspired by non-theistic traditions, *The Rainbow of Faiths*, pp. 63f. Ward goes to meet these types of objections in his significant essay 'Convergent Spirituality', *Christianity in the Twenty-first Century*, ed. Deborah A. Brown, New York: Crossroads 2000.

34 Reproduced in *For All Life*, pp. 52–66.

35 Produced by The Earth Charter Initiative, The Earth Council, Costa Rica, 2000.

36 Reproduced in *Threshold 2000*, p. 108.

37 Steven C. Rockefeller, 'Comment' on Charles Taylor's essay, 'The Politics of Recognition', *Multiculturalism: Examining the Politics of Recognition*, ed. Amy Gutmann, New Jersey: Princeton University Press 1994, p. 92.

8

Interspirituality in the Waiting

'Spirituality' is not easily defined. According to one definition, it 'is a way of life, an active orientation to the world which regulates belief and practice'.[1] Spirituality signifies a sense of personal connectedness with reality and with the intimations of transcendence to be discovered in and through human engagement with reality. In so far as it is the function of religious tradition to nurture a sense of connectedness and transcendence, religions are not only bearers of 'spirituality' they *are* 'spirituality' – or better, 'ways of spirituality'.

In the dialogical context, this holistic definition of spirituality has at least two advantages. First, it rescues religious allegiance from being associated simply with the doctrinal dimension of religion.[2] If religions are simply vehicles for doctrinal interpretations, it follows that the problem of conflicting theologies and philosophies are insuperable, and the possibilities for sharing religious experience negligible. Second, it places the emphasis on our humanity, thus opening the door for the exploration of the religious experience of the other as a human concern. This is significant in more than one way. 'The attempt to enter sympathetically into the spiritual life of other traditions is a vital contribution to human unity,' says Marcus Braybrooke, 'for such meeting is at the deepest level of our being.'[3] It is the sharing of 'transcendent vision and human transformation' across religious party lines that creates the conditions for interreligious dialogue.

This is not to say that spirituality is an introspective matter only. Spirituality as a way of life concerned with connectedness at all levels has been highlighted by the interfaith movement. Robert Muller, former Assistant Secretary-General of the United

Nations, offered the following optimistic picture of the role of religion for future well-being at the second Parliament of the World's Religions:

> The common heritages and institutional authority of the religions, combined with an emerging global spirituality, can make enormous contributions to the challenges and details of creating a better world. Though an atheist, André Malraux has said that 'the third millennium will be spiritual or there will be no third millennium'.[4]

Presumably what this citation is pointing to is not that Christianity, or any other religion or spirituality, can displace politics, science, or commerce, and so on, in the modern world. The secular revolution has happened, and, properly understood, there is no going back on it. But it is the obligation of spirituality (spiritualities!) to ground these human endeavours in a wider sense of connectedness and transcendence. However, if the religions are set to make their renewed contribution towards a better world, it had better be with a sense of self-criticism. For the historic antagonism between the religions is not a legacy that makes for optimism. I would add, therefore, to Muller's invitation that the response of the religions must by necessity be a dialogical one.

This chapter sets out to examine the notion of spirituality as a dialogical challenge for Christian faith.

Comparable Spiritual Fruits and the Language of the Spirit

'Religion', says Iris Murdoch, 'is about the death of the ego. The ego disappears and you see the world with absolute vividness and clarity.'[5] This is a generic appreciation, and suspect therefore for some scholars of religion and theologians. But it is nonetheless capable of being substantiated from the religious traditions themselves. What Murdoch intuits in her novels and writings in terms of psychological, aesthetic and moral experience has been known in religious experience for centuries. So in Christianity, the apostle Paul proclaims: 'I have been crucified with Christ; it is no longer I who live, but Christ who lives in me' (Gal. 2.20a); and in Hinduism, the mystic Shankara expresses the transcending of the ego as union with Brahman: 'The ocean of Brahman is full of nectar – the joy of the Atman';[6] and in Buddhism, followers speak of the experience of *satori* as the loss of the ego in becoming one with the Buddha nature of all reality. The list of examples could be greatly extended.

Of course the expressed content of the religious description of the ego-less state remains resolutely different between the religions. But at the experiential level those who are far advanced on the spiritual quest seem to form what Wayne Teasdale has called a 'fraternity of sages'. As Teasdale has observed:

> Regardless of the tradition, the effects of the spiritual journey on the person are the same. Contemplatives, mystics, and sages, in whatever form of spirituality, undergo a radical refashioning of their being . . . Their consciousness is greatly enhanced and deepened; they acquire a transcendental, subtle awareness. Their character becomes saintly; their will is fixed on love and compassion, mercy and kindness. They are exquisitely sensitive beings, gentle and patient . . .
>
> Such beings exist in all traditions, and are part of a spiritual fraternity of sages that unite all ages and cultures. They are able to appreciate interspiritual wisdom because they are inwardly free . . .[7]

This particular picture draws attention to the goals of the spiritual life as a search in individual experience. Therefore it needs correcting with the reminder that spirituality is also orientated on social and political life. In fact, given that all religious traditions have supported and continue to support whole civilizations, the effects of spiritual fruits expressly take communitarian forms. Teasdale recognizes this when he confirms that 'A viable spirituality today is socially engaged; it does not turn its back on the sufferings of the world, but squarely faces them and contributes to their mitigation and alleviation.' Again, it would be possible to name figures from different traditions to add to the 'fraternity of sages' on this score.

Impressive spirituality elsewhere encountered through friendship, practical collaboration for justice and peace, or sharing cultic experiences, opens up the issue of how 'strange' yet 'resonant' religious experience elsewhere, with its moral and spiritual fruits, relates to the work of the Spirit in Christian experience. Linking the Christian experience of the Spirit with the universal gift of the Spirit encountered in the stranger, Michael Barnes has said that 'a theory of interfaith relations begins not with some vague sense that tolerance is a "good thing" but from a reflection on the moral challenge put to us by the stranger in our midst'.[8] The theme of the stranger in the midst is a compelling one for spirituality, for the stranger is one who has the capacity to enlarge – and perhaps even to alter – the host environment, as a result of his or her own distinctive presence and spiritual gift.

The stranger must be welcomed as one in whom the possibility of God's presence is available. Barnes calls this an 'inclusivist instinct'. Genuine hospitality, he believes, is deeply theological: 'the practice of hospitality should be understood in intrinsically theological terms; it speaks of God in our midst'.[9]

The question arises concerning what kind of theology can accompany this 'inclusivist instinct'? The intention is that we are open to what might turn out to be utterly different and strange when giving hospitality to the stranger. Barnes struggles with the question of whether the spiritual and moral fruits of 'the stranger' can be counted as equal to the Christian instance of them. He simultaneously speaks of Christ as 'the one in whom all human aspirations for unity and intelligibility are brought together', and also of a spiritual 'fullness which is *still to be discovered*'.[10] How these two aspirations can be held together theologically Barnes does not elucidate. There is Christ who reveals God – 'Christ is God's *meaning*' – and there is the Spirit that 'is responsible for the struggles of all people . . . to maintain their own integrity in seeking out and manifesting the mystery of the infinite love of God'.[11] In turning to the future – a fullness '*still to be discovered*' – this suggests an eschatological resolution to the problem. However, Barnes does not develop this possibility. I have noted one version of this possibility above (see p. 46), but pointed out its unsatisfactoriness. Barnes instead appeals to the processes of dialogue and relationships of mutuality between faith-communities, and to the 'Trinitarian mystery' itself. The dialogue of faiths should mirror the dialogue in the heart of the trinitarian God.[12]

Can a trinitarian framework really help? Given the Trinity's prominence in contemporary Christian theology, it seems almost discourteous to suggest a dissenting 'no'. Apart from the vexed question whether or not it is possible to make sense of the doctrine of the Trinity, apart from the fourth- and fifth-century contextual arguments which brought it about, the application of it in the Christian theology of religions has always to face the problem of the supremacy of the revelation of the divine Son in relation to other divine work for which the Spirit may be responsible.

The introduction of a strong emphasis on the work of the Spirit – the so-called pneumatological approach to religious plurality – is said to overcome the difficulties associated with the language of the 'cosmic Christ' or the 'anonymous Christ'. For 'the Spirit blows where it wills' (John 3.8). But what starts out as promising proves less so on closer inspection. This can be illustrated very well from the consultation of a group of international theologians who gathered at Baar in Switzerland in 1990, under the direction of the World Council of Churches. Much of the debate centred on how to extend the language of the Spirit within a trinitarian framework. A key sentence from their final report read:

> We affirm that God has been present in their [the religious traditions] seeking and *finding*, that where there is truth and wisdom in their teachings, and love and holiness in their living, this like any wisdom, insight, knowledge, understanding, love and holiness that is found among us is the gift of the Holy Spirit.[13]

The emphasis on *finding* was a breakthrough, as most official ecclesiastical reports are generally reluctant to admit this level of spiritual comparability between the Christian and other faith-traditions. But the Baar statement was unable to absorb the full implications of its daring move, for in the area of christology it affirmed the orthodox position on Christ:

> We affirm that in Jesus Christ, the incarnate Word, the entire human family has been united to God in an irrevocable bond and covenant. The saving presence of God's activity in all

creation and human history comes to the focal point in the event of Christ.

This seems to me to take back firmly with a second hand what the first hand, equally firmly, had led us initially to expect. What can it mean, in a historically conscious and plural age, for the focal point of all of God's activity, historically and geographically, to cohere in Christ?

Agreeing with a spirit-christology approach to plurality, Jacques Dupuis supports both a trinitarian model, and Barnes, when he says: 'The Christ-event is at the center of the historical unfolding of the divine economy, but the punctual event is actuated and becomes operative throughout time and space in the work of the Spirit.'[14] However, it seems to me that this, again, repeats the dilemma, for it suggests that, if the Christ-event is at the centre, the moral and spiritual fruits of the religions are peripheral to it. Why should we not recognize other 'punctual events'?

Emphasis on the language of the Spirit obviously assists the processes of interfaith dialogue. But in a trinitarian framework it still seems to me to fall short of granting a real independent integrity to other faith-communities, and to do proper justice to the facts and experiences of religious plurality as we now experience them.[15]

Spirituality and the Givenness of Plurality

If comparability between the spiritual fruits of different faith-communities leads Christian faith into strategies and theologies of neighbourliness, then other Christian theologians speak of dialogue with the spirituality of the stranger/neighbour less hesitatingly. In the Asian context, for example, where the overall Christian presence is in the minority, Christian thought is necessarily construed dialogically as a matter of everyday reality.

To take the Indian example, Christian theologians are working on two levels. First, there is the attempt to portray Christian faith in Indian forms. In the liturgical field, and most particularly in Catholic spirituality, liturgical celebration is being adapted to incorporate Indian themes and Indian cultural expressions as vehicles for Christian sensibilities. Readings from Indian scriptures might replace 'the Old Testament', liturgical leaders might wear the clothes of Indian 'holy men' or *sannyasi*, and artistic representations of Jesus as a *sannyasi* may provide a different aesthetic setting for prayer and meditation. This process of 'inculturation' is now accruing a vast literature. But, of course, it cannot proceed without paying serious attention to the religious origins of culture in a context such as India. Inculturation therefore is necessarily dialogical in its method. Some writers consider that not enough serious attention is paid to the theological difficulties of incorporating Indian themes into Christian liturgy and practice.[16]

On the theological level, serious attempts have been made to discover convergence between ancient strands of Indian spirituality and Christian insights.[17] This is not easy, given that the spiritual ethos of Asian-origin religions has been focused on meditative reason, on non-duality, and the Eternal present, whereas the semitic spiritualities of western origin have focused on differentiating reason, duality between subject and object, and the Eternal future. But this has not deterred theologians from spilling much contemplative ink in depicting the *saccidananda*, or being-consciousness-bliss of Nirguna Brahman (the Absolute in itself), as roughly equivalent to the Christian Trinity. 'In Christian *advaita*,' says Jacque Dupuis, 'the Hindu intuition of *saccidananda* and the Christian revelation really converge.'[18] Others explore Indian Hindu concepts and religious traditions as new contexts for expanding Christian faith in fresh ways. For example, M. Thomas Thangaraj has intriguingly examined the possibilities for expressing Jesus in south Indian Tamil culture as a crucified guru.[19] All of these theological experiments begin by acknowledging the religious value of the classical philosophical Indian heritage.

At more popular levels, the gap between the cultural life of most Indian people and Christianity remains wide. As the Jesuit writer, Michael Amaladoss, has said: 'In spite of the existence of certain Asian paths for practicing (*sic*) Asian theology, we continue to repeat the Occidental interpretations and hesitate to express ourselves.' He continues: 'In India most Christians practice (*sic*) their popular religion and lead their daily lives like the other Indians. But, when they come to the liturgical office they become suddenly non-Indian, non-Asian.'[20]

There is another context in Asia that has become dominant in the Christian promotion of dialogical relations with their Hindu, Muslim, Buddhist, and Sikh neighbours. This is the context of poverty. Not only is religious plurality a 'natural' habitat for Christianity in areas such as India, but so is poverty. Given the realities of poverty, the starting-point for Christian witness is turning to interreligious collaboration for the sake of a transformed world. This is leading to the forging of new theologies.

One voice that can be heard above many in Asia is Aloysius Pieris. A Jesuit in Sri Lanka, he is deeply committed to both the liberation of the poor and interreligious dialogue. Indeed, he sees the two movements as integral to the Christian message:

> Inter-religious dialogue and inculturation refer to our mission to *befriend* the poor in their *religiousness* and in their *culture*. It is by such befriending that one learns from God's poor the language of liberation/salvation which Jesus spoke, the language of God's Reign (in whatever name it may be called in various religions).[21]

The religious identity of the Hindu, Buddhist, Jain, and so on, is not valued as a mere stepping-stone, intended to lead followers away from their primary religious roots. Rather, it is that the focus of dialogue and collaboration is the 'option for the poor'. While this is central to Christian faith for Pieris, he also recognizes that other traditions will have their own entry into this shared praxis.

Pieris goes further:

> [T]he 'God–Mammon conflict' is the basis of the *common spirituality* of all religions, even if this spirituality is couched in a non-theistic language in certain religions whereas the 'God–Poor partnership' is a *specifically biblical* message which becomes *distinctively Christian* when it assumes the Jesus-dimension . . .[22]

The reference to a 'common spirituality' will no doubt raise the hackles of the postmoderns who would suspect an illegitimate mixing up of spiritualities here. But Pieris' model does not lead to an uncritical synthesis between religions. Far from it. Christian faith is a distinctive witness within the dialogue which keeps alive the 'option for the poor' and prophetically challenges Buddhists, Hindus, and others, to act out of their own distinctive liberative resources. But there is also a 'mutual discipleship' bound up with a 'common spirituality', and this opens Christians up to attend also to the message of the religious other. It is almost as if the 'thick'–'thin' distinction that I noted in discussion with a Global Ethic (see above, p. 130) applies here also. The 'thin' commonality is the shared spirituality of the 'God–Mammon' conflict at the heart of economic, social and political relationships, and the 'thick' theology is the distinctive differences the religions bring to bear on one another and the world in dialogical exchange and mutual critique.

Pieris' vision is one of the most articulated in the Asian context. It provides a defence against those who would complain that interfaith dialogue based on the mutual valuing of different traditions leads to indifference in terms of ethical or theological commitment. Pieris' is a committed vision.

Asian voices are claiming to steer the debate over the Christian theology of religions in new directions, and this raises a further consideration within the terms of reference of this book. It is this: Asian liberation theologians are expressing weariness with the exclusive-inclusive-pluralist typology of western debate. 'I have found myself gradually appropriating a trend in Asia,' noted Pieris in 1993, 'which adopts a paradigm wherein the three categories . . . [Exclusivism, Inclusivism, Pluralism] do not make sense.'[23] And Michael Amaladoss complains: 'The problem with [those] who talk about the experience of religious pluralism in the categories of exclusivism, inclusivism, and pluralism is that sometimes they do not rise beyond the horizontal and phenomenological level of the historians of religions.'[24]

In so far as the threefold typology does not address directly the contextual poverty of much of Asia this complaint seems reasonable. However, this is not grounds for rejecting the typology altogether. Advocating interreligious collaboration for the sake of alleviating poverty, coupled with the acceptance of the authentic value of the many religions, does seem to imply a

'pluralistic instinct' (to adapt Michael Barnes' terminology).
Pieris himself designates 'common ground' when he signals
'Obedience and Poverty as a Universal Spirituality'. All religions,
he admits, share an 'irrevocable commitment to an Ultimate
horizon of absolute freedom . . . coupled with a radical renunci-
ation of all that stands in its way' as that which is 'universally
accepted in all religions and expressed in various ways, sometimes even in non-theistic terms'.[25] This is of the essence of
Christian faith, believes Pieris, but it can also be found in other
faith-traditions.

As further evidence of the 'pluralist instinct', consider also the
following position from Asia:

> The religions of the world are expressions of the human open-
> ness to God. They are signs of God's presence in the world.
> Every religion is unique and through this uniqueness, religions
> enrich one another. In their specificity, they manifest different
> faces of the supreme Mystery which is never exhausted. In
> their diversity, they enable us to experience the richness of the
> One more profoundly. When religions encounter one another
> in dialogue, they build up a community in which differences
> become complementarities and divergences are changed into
> pointers to communion.[26]

This Statement was made as part of seeking to distance an Asian
view from the perceived western 'theoretical approaches to the
faith of other people'. But it seems to me a very good basic
outline of a pluralist position endorsed in this book. Moreover,
it is endorsed, not simply as a result of analysis at the 'phenomenological level of the historians of religions', as Amaladoss
would have it. But it is a committed position based in Christian
faith, yet wholly open to the authenticity of the Other and
lacking any hint of Christian superiority.

The real challenge from accepting the authenticity of plural
voices is to Christian orthodoxy. Liberationist concerns –
wholly understandable and incontestable coming from Asian
settings – redirect the focus, as it were, of Christian belief in the
incarnation and Trinity, beliefs that lie in the doctrinal background of liberationist concerns. The shift is away from pre-
occupation with purely theoretical and scholastic definitions

towards their potential meaning for the liberation of society. The basic doctrinal affirmation is left in tact.

But the basic doctrinal pattern remains as a contested site in its own right. This is made clear in Amaladoss's warning against Paul Knitter's reinterpretation of christology (see above p. 76): 'If God is the Trinity, however this is understood, and if the Second Person of the blessed Trinity became a human person, however this process is explained, then that person is not just unique as any other human person or spiritual leader is unique.'[27] The liberationists cannot have it both ways – by assuming Christian orthodoxy as given and applying it to inter-religious dialogue as though that were unproblematic. For if the affirmation of the incarnation and Trinity is 'uniquely different' from all others, then, as Amaladoss has correctly discerned, it leads to the eventual superiority of the Christian outlook. The latter may be downplayed in dialogue with Asian religions, for the sake of dialogue and collaboration in the midst of poverty, but the theological challenge remains.

Complementarity or What?

Religions as spiritualities, ways of life seeking a vision of transcendence and human transformation, are both integrated life-orientations, cross-linked in every dimension (ethics, doctrine, experiential etc), and open-ended, dynamic move-ments that have borrowed from many facets of culture and changed through time. These features exist in continual tension, first propelling religions together and then tearing them apart.

Support for the view of incommensurability stems from the phenomenology of religious experience. To find a point of 'sameness' therefore across great and small divides seems hopelessly idealistic.

But what about claims for a mystical unity among the religions? The classic writer on religious experience, William James, said that the 'overcoming of all the usual barriers between the individual and the Absolute is the great mystic achievement. In mystic states we both become one with the Absolute and we are aware of our oneness.'[28] Does this mean that mystics have similar experiences but interpret them differently, according to the spiritual tradition in which they have been nurtured? The situation is probably more complicated than this analysis allows. For it would seem that the interpretative framework of religious tradition itself already makes its own contribution to the structuring of experience. So Christian mystics have 'Christian' experiences and Buddhists 'Buddhist' experiences, and so on. In other words, the different accounts of mystical experiences from different traditions declare characteristically different descriptions of the unitive state and of Ultimate Reality.[29] Religions are different.

On the other hand, approaches that have allowed themselves to be influenced by dialogical riches, present a different perspective. Dialogue breaks boundaries. Religions may be different, but that should not necessarily confine them to separate boxes. They have interacted through history; they have changed shape through the centuries and across cultures.[30] Julius Lipner says of religions that they are 'syncretic realities, the complex result of countless transcultural conceptual, linguistic etc. overlappings, compromises, interactings', which not surprisingly create the conditions for spiritual bonds across great divides, such as that which transpired between Thomas Merton and the Dalai Lama. As he says: '[Interfaith spirituality] is possible because there seem to be no sustainable a priori objections to its occurrence, and because it has occurred and continues to occur (as testimony from the lives of spiritual practitioners indicates) in the history of religions.'[31]

Philip Novak has pointed out that there may be anthropological roots to this possibility for interspiritual dialogue. He cites the sociobiologist E. O. Wilson's approval of G. P. Murdock's list of fifty-eight cultural universals, and draws the conclusion that across different cultural groups 'Psychic unity . . . is . . . a fact.' And further, from Wilson: 'the predisposition to religious belief is the most complex and powerful force in the human mind and in all probability an ineradicable part of human nature'.[32] These tendencies to universality in the human race lead Novak to propose that the religions of the future should 'seek a theological universal in a common *function* of God and God-equivalents' in order to engender the age-old religious vocation to live in alignment with a sense of cosmic order. This universal would be a 'tract of conceptual land belonging to everyone and owned by no one, where universes of discourse can meet and make common cause'.[33]

The extent to which one can derive theological principles from anthropological observations is a moot point. Nevertheless, Novak's reliance on anthropology and cultural observations does open the door to the search for commonalities among the religions. His suggestion of a functional spiritual common ground echoes what has already been suggested in this book in relation to ethical and theological discussion.

The functional common ground has in fact been observed and to a degree confirmed through dialogue itself. Appendix 2 indicates the agreement reached in monastic dialogue. It is a functional agreement, to be sure, but manifesting an impressive range of overlap. In commenting on the dialogical fruits, Thomas Keating, one of the prime movers behind the monastic dialogue, is not naive about what can be derived from such experiences: 'Whether or not the ultimate experience of God in this life is the same in the world religions, the spiritual paths to the experience of unity are clearly not the same.'[34] He agrees, however, that it does provide the means for mutuality between and for learning from different spiritual practices. Furthermore, he accepts that it is possible for some people to occupy two different worldviews and communities simultaneously – Christian and Buddhist, or Christian and Hindu etc. – but these will be the exceptions, not the rule.

The question that arises most naturally is how to account *religiously* for such diversity among the religions and yet convergence at levels of moral and spiritual fruits of religious experience. What theory of interreligious relations does justice to the facts of experience? Exclusivism and Inclusivism, in their different ways, assume that the way of Christ is the final path of spiritual access to the truth of Ultimate Reality, to be realized in this life or in a post-mortem existence. But there is no empirical backing for this assumption; indeed the evidence points in the opposite direction. Christianity has produced its saints and holy figures – monastic-quietist or political-activist – but so have the other traditions.

We should not say that the religions worship the same

Ultimate Reality, for the descriptions of that Reality from the different traditions do not seem to show sufficient compatibility. The Christian description of 'God our Father' is not the same as 'Allah the all-merciful and all-compassionate', or as the 'boundless openness' of Mahayana Buddhism, and so on. Neither, as I pointed out above, is it promising to adopt a simple 'common experience' model of earlier interpretations of the phenomenology of religious experience and mysticism. This is not to say that religious experiences do not have much in common. There are many experiences that can be classified according to common criteria, such as 'enlightenment', 'compassion', 'the void', to use some of the categories from one interesting collection.[35] The real question is how to account for the diversity of interpretations of religious experience, both by those who undergo them and by the religious traditions themselves.

Religious experience, according to classic texts and trained mystics, is highly structured according to particular traditions. But it does not automatically follow from this that differently structured religious experiences do not necessarily derive from the one Ultimate Reality. As a result of work with the Religious Experience Research Unit, David Hay has commented that

> [The] powerful structuring of the interpretation of experience doesn't lead us to deny the reality of a common ground for it, any more than differences in language between people from different countries lead us to say that, in more than a metaphorical sense, they don't inhabit the same world as us.[36]

Hay admits that this view is not very popular with professional students of religion. But his point does have some credence. It would benefit from a tighter philosophical framework that properly clarifies the status of the common ground and its relationship with the phenomenological differences between religions.

One recent suggestion of a framework along these lines has been made by Keith Ward, in his notion of 'convergent spirituality'. Ward accepts that 'In religion, as in all other spheres of human knowledge, truth must be one, though access to it, and perspectives on it, may be diverse.'[37] He is clear that a religious tradition is grounded in the experience of its founder, and that critical approaches in theology and philosophy mean that 'The many religions of the world are not simply or primarily competing philosophical systems. They are metaphorical or symbolic systems encoding paradigmatic forms of spiritual experience, experience leading to liberation.'[38] As an illustration of how this applies across traditions, Ward examines the main thrust of the Christian and Buddhist worlds, and accepts that 'Both experiences may be of the same reality, which, though in itself possessing a certain form of simplicity, has many complex facets in relation to finite beings.'[39] This complexity, combined with the limitations of human culture, leads to endless argumentation at the level of doctrinal discussion, but at the level of liberating experience there is the possibility of a convergent spirituality. Partial back-up for this assessment from a tradition point of view can be found in the overtures that each tradition, Christian and Buddhist, makes towards its opposite. So Christian history has a strand of unitive mysticism within it where God is not addressed in personal terms and Buddhism would appreciate this; and Buddhism contains strands which acknowledge personal aspects of the eternal Buddha-nature (*Dharmakaya*), a factor that would interest Christianity. In other words, there is a tendency towards convergence.

Ward's highly suggestive outlook is almost indistinguishable from the religious philosophical appreciation of plurality developed by John Hick (see p. 30f.). Ward has been critical of Hick,[40] but the essential elements of 'convergent spirituality' seem to be in reasonably close agreement with him. Both writers accept the distinction between the 'eternal' aspects of a religion and its metaphorical 'face' in human language and history. Both appeal for their assessment of the power of religion to the formative religious experience of a founder. Both believe that the same spiritual reality underlies different paradigmatic experiences. Both agree that 'To say that those paths converge on one and the same reality and goal is not to say that they are the same, or that they are all equally direct and sure, or that there is little to choose among them.'[41]

Perhaps the main differences between the two occur chiefly in the area of christology. Ward retains a more-or-less orthodox version of the incarnation, whereas Hick proposes a metaphorical view.[42] In my own reading of the issues, it seems that Hick has brought into the open the real difference between the two positions. The orthodox view of Christ entails that the Christian faith ought to lead to a superior history of moral and spiritual endeavour than found in other faith-traditions, for it supposes that 'God-in-person' was responsible in some sense for founding the Christian faith. The metaphorical/symbolic view, on the other hand, accepts that Jesus embodies the compassion and goodness of God as a symbol of what God intends for all peoples. Again, for reasons given above (Chapter 4), I find the greater consistency with the general positive appreciation of plurality to be found in the metaphorical/symbolic interpretation of Jesus and his impact.

Ward's vision is one of convergence; Hick's is of complementarity. This latter view is more definite philosophically about the validity of independent ways of spirituality in relation to Ultimate Reality. So Hick's distinction between the Real *an sich* (Ultimate Reality in itself) and the 'personae' and 'impersonae' (the manifestations in human consciousness and varied spiritual life) of the Real provides a substantial philosophical framework for explaining religious plurality alongside the ultimate 'unity' of That Which can only remain eternal mystery.

The celebrated Vietnamese Buddhist mystic, scholar and activist, Thich Nhat Hanh, has captured both the resonance and the strangeness between religions that have occupied the central concerns of this book. In his meditations on Jesus and Buddha, he unites the two figures when he writes:

> Jesus had the power to bring joy, happiness, and healing to others because the energy of the Holy Spirit was full inside him. We [Buddhists] have the seed of the Holy Spirit in us. In the Buddhist circle we speak of Buddhahood. We speak of mindfulness . . .[43]

The writer feels no awkwardness in borrowing the language of 'Holy Spirit' for Buddhist purposes, thereby realizing a bond of experience between two religious worlds. But Hanh feels the strangeness of the two traditions when he also writes: 'The image of Jesus that is presented to us is unusually of Jesus on the cross. This is a very painful image for me. It does not convey joy or peace, and this does not do justice to Jesus.'[44] Just at the point where many Christians feel drawn to the centre of their faith – in the cross – the Buddhist steps back. Is it possible to reconcile these two attitudes? Hanh asks for 'Buddhist' portrayals of Jesus – as a walking meditator or as an ascetic sitting in the meditative lotus position – in order to ease the pain of difference. These will have their validity, but they do not really reconcile two religious apprehensions of life that seem irreconcilable at the experiential level.

Commenting on the radical differences between the two large-scale claims of 'ultimacy' on us – the personal theistic awareness and the transpersonal unitive awareness – Wayne Teasdale also believes in the complementarity view:

> God is both a loving presence, compassionate, wise, kind, and merciful, and an impersonal principle or ultimate condition of consciousness, the basis of karma *shunyata* or emptiness, and *nirvana*. They represent two sides of the same source, two fundamental insights, two mystical realizations of the ultimate mystery.[45]

Teasdale has not expressed himself with sufficient philosophical subtlety in speaking of 'God' as the ultimate mystery for all traditions. However, once this terminological correction is made, the future as one of 'interspirituality' in mutual respect, critical dialogue, shared experiences and collaboration between the traditions seems a destiny that awaits us. It is an idealistic vision. But it is also, as Teasdale says: 'the foundation that can prepare the way for a planet-wide enlightened culture, and a continuing community among the religions that is substantial, vital, and creative'.[46]

Notes

1 Julius Lipner, 'The "Inter" of Interfaith Spirituality', *Interfaith Spirituality*, The Way Supplement 78, 1993, p. 66; cf. the definition from Wayne Teasdale, *The Mystic Heart: Discovering a Universal Spirituality in the World's Religions*, California: New World Library 1999, p. 17: '*Spirituality* is a way of life that affects and includes every moment of

existence. It is at once a contemplative attitude, a disposition to a life of depth, and the search for ultimate meaning, direction, and belonging.'

2 Cf. Keith Ward: 'Religion is about spirituality not doctrine', 'Convergent Spirituality', *Christianity in the Twenty-First Century*, ed. Deborah A. Brown, New York: Crossroad 2000, p. 70.

3 Marcus Braybrooke, *Faith and Interfaith in a Global Age*, Grand Rapids: CoNexus Press and Oxford: Braybrooke Press 1998, pp. 117f.

4 Robert Muller, 'Preparing for the Next Millennium,' *A Sourcebook for Earth's Community of Religions*, ed. Joel Beversluis, Grand Rapids: CoNexus Press and New York: Global Education Associates, revised edition, 2000, p. 3.

5 Ronald S. Lello (ed.), *Revelations: Glimpses of Reality*, London: Shepheard-Walwyn Ltd. and Border Television Plc 1985, pp. 88f.

6 Cited by John Hick, *The Fifth Dimension: An Exploration of the Spiritual Realm*, Oxford: Oneworld 1999, p. 176.

7 Wayne Teasdale, *The Mystic Heart: Discovering a Universal Spirituality in the World's Religions*, California: New World Library 1999, p. 102.

8 Michael Barnes, 'On Not Including Everything', *Interfaith Spirituality*, The Way Supplement 78, 1993, p. 7.

9 Michael Barnes, 'Practising God's Hospitality', *World Faiths Encounter* 27 (November 2000), p. 12.

10 Barnes, 'Practising God's Hospitality', p. 9.

11 Barnes, 'Practising God's Hospitality', p. 11.

12 See his *Religions in Conversation*, London: SPCK 1989, p. 152: 'The interfaith dialogue actually mirrors the life of the Trinity.'

13 The Baar Statement, with the conference papers and responses, can be found in the publication of the World Council of Churches, *Current Dialogue* 19 (January 1991). Italics mine.

14 Jacques Dupuis SJ, *Toward a Christian Theology of Religious Pluralism*, Maryknoll: Orbis Books 1997, p. 207.

15 See my *Christians and Religious Pluralism*, London: SCM Press, second edition, 1993, pp. 156–58, for further consideration of the Trinity in the theology of religions. For an alternative view, see Rowan Williams, 'Trinity and Pluralism', *Christian Uniqueness Reconsidered: The Myth of a Pluralistic Theology of Religions*, ed. Gavin D'Costa, Maryknoll: Orbis Books 1990, chapter 1.

16 For example, Lipner, 'The 'Inter' of Interfaith Spirituality', p. 67; cf. M. Zago OC, 'India: the Challenge of Inculturation', *Mission Outlook*, Winter 1990, p. 128: 'The local religious and cultural expressions are so strong and deeply rooted that the Christian presence must inculturate itself if it is not to appear as an extraneous body or foreign institution. But this inculturation becomes problematic and difficult on account of the cultural and religious differences of the country.'

17 The writings of Bede Griffiths, for example, are dominated by this classic concern: see *The Marriage of East and West*, London: Fount Paperbacks 1983, and *A New Vision of Reality: Western Science, Eastern Mysticism and Christian Faith*, London: HarperCollins, Fount 1989.

18 Dupuis, *Toward a Christian Theology of Religious Pluralism*, p. 279. But notice his differentiation of 'intuition' from 'revelation'. Is there a hint of hierarchical value here? Cf. the imaginative attempt at convergence by John A. T. Robinson, *Truth is Two-Eyed*, London: SCM Press 1979.

19 M. Thomas Thangaraj, *The Crucified Guru: An Experiment in Cross-Cultural Christology*, Nashville: Abingdon 1994; cf. Anton Wessels, *Images of Jesus: How Jesus is Perceived and Portrayed in Non-European Cultures*, London: SCM Press 1990.

20 Michael Amaladoss, L'Église d'Asie parle de pluralisme à partir de son expérience', *Églises d'Asie*, 16 Avril 1997, p. 22. Cited by O. Degryse CICM, *Interreligious Dialogue: The Asian Churches Set the Tone*, Louvain 1999, p. 85.

21 Aloysius Pieris SJ, *God's Reign for God's Poor: a Return to the Jesus Formula*, Tulana Research Centre, Sri Lanka, second revised edition, 1999, p. 67.

22 Pieris, *God's Reign for God's Poor*, p. 69; cf. Walter Fernandes of the Indian Social Institute, Delhi: 'To evolve a liberation theology, persons of different religious traditions would have to search for the prophetic elements in the context of their common option to support those who are struggling to free themselves from oppression.' Cited by Paul F. Knitter in *One Earth, Many Religions: Multifaith Dialogue and Global Responsibility*, Maryknoll: Orbis Press 1995, pp. 158f.

23 Aloysius Pieris SJ, 'An Asian Paradigm: Interreligious Dialogue and Theology of Religions, *Month* 26, 1993, pp. 129–34.

24 Michael Amaladoss SJ, 'A Simple Solution', *The Uniqueness of Jesus: A Dialogue with Paul F. Knitter*, ed. Leonard Swidler and Paul Mojzes, Maryknoll: Orbis Press 1997, p. 27.

25 Pieris, *God's Reign for God's Poor*, p. 37.

26 Statement from the Thirteenth Annual Meeting of the Indian Theological Association (1989), held under the title 'Towards an Indian Christian Theology of Religious Pluralism', *Religious Pluralism: An Indian Christian Perspective*, ed. K. Pathil, Delhi: ISPCK 1991. The Statement is cited by Dupuis as 'evidence' of a changing view in Asia towards welcoming plurality 'not merely as a matter of fact but in principle' (p. 201); cf. Pieris' complementary picture between 'Christian agape' and 'Buddhist gnosis', which exist in 'indefinable contrast', yet also 'must be recognized . . . as necessary precisely because each in itself is inadequate as a medium not only for experiencing but also for expressing our intimate moments with the Ultimate Source of liberation.' See his 'The Buddha

and the Christ: Mediators of Liberation', *Asian Faces of Jesus*, ed. R. S. Sugirtharajah, London: SCM Press 1993, p. 47.

27 Amaladoss, 'A Simple Solution', p. 26.

28 William James, *The Varieties of Religious Experience* (1902), London: Collins Fount 1979, p. 404.

29 The details of the argument can be found in Steven T. Katz, 'Language, Epistemology, and Mysticism', *Mysticism and Philosophical Analysis*, ed. Steven T. Katz, New York: Oxford University Press 1978, pp. 22–74.

30 Cf. Wilfred Cantwell Smith, *Towards a World Theology: Faith and the Comparative History of Religion*, London and Basingstoke: Macmillan Press 1981, chapter 1.

31 Lipner, 'The "Inter" of Interfaith Spirituality', p. 68.

32 E. O. Wilson, *On Human Nature*, New York: Bantam 1982, p. 176. Cited in Philip Novak, 'Universal Theology and the Idea of Cosmic Order', *World Faiths Encounter* 2 (July 1992), p. 5.

33 Novak, 'Universal Theology', p. 4.

34 Thomas Keating, 'Theological Issues in Meditative Technologies', *Interfaith Spirituality*, The Way Supplement 78, 1993, p. 59.

35 J. M. Cohen and J-F. Phipps, *The Common Experience* London: Rider and Company 1979.

36 David Hay, *Religious Experience Today; Studying the Facts*, London: Mowbray Cassell 1990, p. 64; cf. his *Exploring Inner Space: Is God Still Possible in the Twentieth Century?*, Oxford: Mowbray, revised edition, 1987.

37 Ward, 'Convergent Spirituality', p. 68.

38 Ward, 'Convergent Spirituality', pp. 68f.

39 Ward, 'Convergent Spirituality', p. 65.

40 See his articles 'Divine Ineffability', *God, Truth and Reality: Essays in Honour of John Hick*, ed. Arvind Sharma, Basingstoke: Macmillan Press 1993, and 'Truth and the Diversity of Religions', *Religious Studies* 26, no. 1, March 1990; cf. Hick's responses to his critics in *The Rainbow of Faiths: Critical Dialogue on Religious Pluralism*, London: SCM Press 1995, and published as *A Christian Theology of Religions*, Louisville KY: Westminster/John Knox 1995.

41 Ward, 'Convergent Spirituality', pp. 69f.

42 Cf. Keith Ward, *Religion and Revelation: A Theology of Revelation in the World's Religions*, Oxford: Clarendon Press 1994, part IV; and John Hick, *The Metaphor of God Incarnate*: London: SCM Press 1993.

43 Thich Nhat Hanh, *Going Home: Jesus and Buddha as Brothers*, London: Rider Books 1999, p. 46.

44 Hanh, *Going Home*, p. 46.

45 Teasdale, *The Mystic Heart*, p. 26.

46 Teasdale, *The Mystic Heart*, p. 26.

9

Some Concluding Remarks

Global awareness entails that the religiously committed can no longer imagine their particular religion alone holds the key to the meaning of life and the truth about Ultimate Reality. The sheer fact of encounter with the religious other disturbs any complacency about the givenness and finality or absolutism of one's own position.

This disturbance is nicely illustrated in a passage from the novel *The Book of Lights*, by the Jewish writer Chaim Potok, to which I first alluded in my Introduction (see p. xi). Following his first 'culture shock' that the religion in which he was nurtured did not seem relevant in an entirely different cultural setting, the hero, Gershon, and his companion, John, undergo a further shock. While walking down a street, they stumble across a Shinto shrine. Gershon notices all the trappings of religious practice – prayers being said by the faithful, candles burning, an altar with an image on it. Then he ponders an old man who is praying, obviously according to Shinto rituals, and falls into conversation about the scene:

> 'Do you think our God is listening to him, John?'
> 'I don't know, chappy. I never thought of it.'
> 'Neither did I until now. If He's not listening, why not? If He is listening, then – well, what are *we* all about, John?'[1]

For the most part, the otherness of the praying Shinto stranger encountered by Gershon in Potok's novel is both terrifying and compelling for spiritual reasons. It is terrifying because the otherness of the praying stranger does not conform to what is already religiously known in Gershon's Jewish tradition, and yet the piety of the stranger is genuine. Could God be so mean as not to listen? On the other hand, the praying man is compelling because it is Gershon's suspicion that the Jewish tradition's open-endedness – God's surprises, God's independence even from his designated chosen people, his providential propensity for being present with other peoples and cultures (as the scriptures have often said) – should lead him to attend to the spiritual message that is hidden in the enactment of the strange ritual itself. The novel's story-line could easily be translated into Christian terms, and have the same impact. What are *we* all about?

The religions face one another as never before. How are we to respond? I have sought to address this question with the aid of the metaphor of twin tracks. Track One represents the search for a theologically satisfying answer to the realities of religious plurality. Track Two takes seriously the adventure of dialogue as a process that harbours a new understanding of religious truth. In negotiating the twin tracks, Christian theologians have perhaps been in the vanguard of a struggle that is taking place in religious living and believing across the traditions.

But the Christian experiment so far has also exposed a deeply troubling scene. Along Track One, Christian theological absolutism is profoundly challenged by the facts and experiences of plurality. It does not seem plausible to advocate Christian supremacy in the face of the impressiveness of 'transcendent vision and human transformation' in many places and times. Is 'our God' listening? 'Yes' – so: what, then, are we all about? The answer is: in transition to a new paradigm for doing theology and living religiously. Answers which refuse to admit that other religions bring anything new to our understanding of the meaning of life and ultimate truth fly in the face not only of common sense but also of the universalist Christian expectation that God is not left without witnesses. Answers which fold the truth of other faith-communities into a greater Christian understanding end up, in effect, subsuming the experience of others under the Christian banner. Hence I contend that the hypothesis which best corresponds to our new global awareness is that represented by a pluralist hypothesis.

Along Track Two, the momentum of interfaith dialogue in many forms is generating a 'new way of thinking' about the nature of religious commitment and identity. Encounter through dialogue has the potential to move through at least three stages: (1) facing the truth about the religious other and oneself, beyond stereotyping the other and with self-criticism; (2) tolerating a different religious worldview as authentic in its own right and leading to a form of parallel living; (3) accepting that the movement beyond fixed positions summons everyone to a new relationship of interactive communion. In the dialogue loop, believing without absolutes might seem an odd prospect.[2]

Believing with a multiplicity of absolutes seems equally strained. But believing with a critical sense of one's hold on the absolute, because it is from within a limited human point of view (what other view is there?), leads one to be open to others who also have their hold on the absolute in equally limited ways. This is the openness that promotes more fruitful dialogue. The pluralist position in the Christian theology of religions supports this view of dialogue, believing that this perspective does better justice to the rationale and fruits of dialogue than any other position.

Those who remain unconvinced are left with the uncomfortable position where the twin tracks of interfaith encounter remain in unresolved tension. Though he has contributed enormously to the interfaith endeavour, Hans Küng illustrates this tension well, and he is worth citing fully:

Seen from the outside, as it were considered in terms of the study of religions, there are of course different true religions . . . There are different ways of salvation (with different saving figures) towards the one goal, which can even partly overlap and which at all events can mutually fructify one another.

Seen from the inside, i.e. from the standpoint of believing Christians orientated on the New Testament, and thus for me, as someone who is affected and challenged, there is only one true God as he has made himself known in Jesus Christ. However, the one true religion in no way excludes truth in other religions, but can allow their validity: with qualifications they are true religions (in this sense 'conditioned' or in some way 'true'). In so far as they do not directly contradict the Christian message, other religions can supplement and correct Christian religion and make it more profound.[3]

Küng calls these, respectively, 'outside' and 'inside' perspectives. The strain between them is obvious, as can be noted from the awkwardness of the language of 'conditioned' and 'in some way "true"'. Yet in so far as we are aware of the limitations of our religious symbolic language what can it mean to assume that Christian faith (or any other) is 'the one true religion'? Encounter in dialogue assumes that we approach one another not simply as students of the scientific study of religion but as committed people. In the dialogue we are all insiders! We are all 'in some way "true"'; and we all seek to 'mutually fructify one another'. Not insiders and outsiders, useful as that distinction might be for some purposes; but people informed variously but in communion together – as Cantwell Smith used to say, 'a "we all" talking together about "us"'.⁴

This book has not sought to examine every nook and cranny of the struggle to understand the relationship between the twin tracks of interfaith encounter. It has not engaged seriously, for example, with so-called religious Fundamentalism, or with the evangelistic dynamics of Christian mission, or with feminist discussions of plurality, or with non-realist theological positions.⁵ It has concentrated on a fairly single-minded quest: to see whether it is possible to discover any points at which the twin tracks of interfaith encounter might intersect. On the whole, it has to be admitted that in much Christian theology the twin tracks remain firmly separated.

This leads me to conclude by asking what options might be open to Christians faced with the demands of religious plurality. There seem to be the following:

1 Christian Fundamentalism, which itself is partly a reaction against the development of positive approaches to religious plurality. But Fundamentalism is a drawbridge mentality that refuses to face up to facts.

2 A compound mentality, sometimes called postmodern, which believes in celebrating difference and is therefore prepared to forage outside the compound from time to time. But this position also refuses to ponder whether or not faith-traditions, *as traditions* in their own right, participate in the impact of Ultimate Reality in the world as part of a greater

understanding of our global religious environment. Therefore this position too seems a half-hearted response.

3 A don't know attitude, which is prepared to promote dialogical awareness of others and tolerance of others (because of a genuine humility about the human propensity to know), but not engage theologically or philosophically in the big picture. While there is much to commend this epistemological humility, at the end of the day this attitude fails to satisfy because our religious symbols, in critical-realist thinking, do claim to embody at least something of the inkling of the truth of Ultimate Reality that corresponds to our experience. The search for the big picture, therefore, should not be abandoned.

4 A stance that retains Christian absolutism (i.e. Christ as the final truth), believing its loss to be detrimental to the Christian outlook, but grants theological space to other visions and other absolutisms, and welcomes a continuing process of friendship, exchange and dialogue for the sake of a dynamic view of religious life and mutual learning. This is a common position, but without letting go of the absolutism at its core, it is hard to know how to avoid the inconsistency it portrays.

5 A view similar to the last position, but pushing towards the pluralist option by limiting the absolute demand inherent in commitment to one's own community of faith. That is to say, allegiance to Christ is absolute for the Christian (and other) community only as a matter of personal commitment. 'It is a recognition that deep religious commitment is necessarily felt as absolute,' Harold Coward explains, 'and as such functions as the validating criterion for all of one's personal experience. This however, does not impose it on others or rule out the recognition that in other persons there is a similar absolute commitment to a particular experience, which will be different from one's own.'[6] Philosophers of religion, and others, will point out that a psychological explanation of absolutism does not do proper justice to the nature of religious truth itself. A religion is not true only 'for me', but also 'for everyone else'. It may be better to clarify further the use of the language of religious absolutism.

6 A variation of the previous position, but which accepts both

that all religious worldviews which have stood the test of time reflect a genuine experience of Ultimate Reality and that the language of absolutism is best put to one side. Christianity is 'in touch' with Ultimate Reality through its particular articulation of theism, but there is no need to pretend to present that as final or superior. But other traditions too are 'in touch' with Ultimate Reality through their particular symbol systems and histories. Christian faith is 'true for me' as an insight into reality, but not as an absolute.[7] Dialogue is welcome as the road towards a more complex view of religious truth on a global scale. This is the pluralist position.

Let Rosemary Ruether spell out the big picture that results from this approach to the twin tracks of theology and dialogue:

> True universality lies in accepting one's own finiteness, one's own particularity and, in so doing, not making that particularity the only true faith, but allowing other particularities to stand side by side with yours as having equal integrity. Each is limited and particular, and yet each is, in its own way, an adequate way of experiencing the whole for a particular people at a particular time.[8]

I would add that while different faith-traditions are each 'an adequate way of experiencing the whole', this picture needs supplementing with the summons to dialogue and mutual learning. In dialogue, we offer our truths but not our absolutisms in a critical relationship that does not claim eventual superiority for my tradition. Dialogue as a 'new way of thinking' stimulates not rivalry but communion: any one community's apprehension of religious truth will be truth that exists for all, and is to be appropriated within a dialogical framework. It seems to me that it is the pluralist hypothesis that best supports this global religious goal.

Notes

1 Chaim Potok, *The Book of Lights*, London: Penguin Books 1983, p. 248.

2 Cf. Reinhold Bernhardt, *Christianity Without Absolutes*, London: SCM Press 1994.

3 Hans Küng, *Global Responsibility: In Search of a New World Ethic*, London: SCM Press 1991, p. 99f.

4 Wilfred Cantwell Smith, *Towards a World Theology: Faith and the Comparative History of Religion*, London and Basingstoke; Macmillan Press 1981, p. 101.

5 Cf. David Hart, *One Faith? Non-Realism and the World of Faiths*, London: Mowbray Cassell 1995.

6 Harold Coward, 'Religious Pluralism and the Future of Religions', *Religious Pluralism and Truth*, Thomas Dean, SUNY 1995, pp. 6of.

7 For those worried by the relativistic shape of this view, cf. the remark of Stanley Samartha: 'Pluralism does not relativize *Truth*. It relativizes different *responses* to Truth which are conditioned by history and culture', Stanley J. Samartha, *Between Two Cultures: Ecumenical Ministry in a Pluralistic World*, Geneva: WCC 1996, p. 190.

8 'Feminism and Jewish-Christian Dialogue: Particularism and Universalism in the Search for Religious Truth', *The Myth of Christian Uniqueness: Toward a Pluralistic Theology of Religions*, eds. John Hick and Paul F. Knitter, Maryknoll: Orbis Press 1987 and London: SCM Press 1988, p. 142.

Appendix 1

THE DIALOGUE DECALOGUE

The Global Dialogue Institute, Philadelphia 2000
Founder-Directors:
Professor Leonard Swidler, Temple University, Philadelphia, USA
Professor Ashok Gangadean, Haverford College, Philadelphia, USA

Ground Rules of Personal and Communal Deep-Dialogue/Critical-Thinking

1 Be open within.
Open our self to our dialogue partner so as to learn, that is, to change and grow in our perception and understanding of reality, and then act accordingly – a self-critical-thinking, intra-personal move.

2 Attend.
Be fully present both to our self and our partner in a critical-thinking mode; respond to our partner rather than make our favourite speech.

3 Be open between.
Make dialogue a two-sided project – within each community as well as between communities – a critical-thinking, inter-communal move.

4 Be honest and trusting.
Come to the dialogue with complete honesty and sincerity, that is, in a critical-thinking mode.
Conversely: assume a similar complete honesty and sincerity – critical-thinking – in our partner.

5 Cultivate personal trust.
Cultivate personal trust by searching first for commonalities, since dialogue can take place only on the basis of mutual trust.

6 Don't prejudge; compare fairly.

   Come to the dialogue with no hard-and-fast assumptions as to where the points of agreement and disagreement are.

   At the same time: compare our ideals with our partner's ideals, our practice with our partner's practice.

7 Define yourself – in dialogue.

   We and our partner define ourselves in dialogue.

8 Treat others as equals.

   Treat our partner as an equal, for dialogue and self-critical-thinking can take place only between equals.

9 Be healthily self-critical.

   Be healthily self-critical of our self and our group or community; only then can we be compassionately critical of our partner.

10 Pass over and return.

   Pass over and experience our partner's community or tradition 'from within', and then return to our own, enriched.

   Source: 'The Technology of Deep-Dialogue/Critical Thinking', Global Dialogue Institute, Temple University, Philadelphia, USA.

Some other sources for 'rules' of dialogue, include:

Martin Buber, 'Six Criteria for Authentic Dialogue', cited by Rami Mark Shapiro, 'Moving the Fence: One Rabbi's View of Interreligious Dialogue', *Inter-Religious Dialogue: Voices from a New Frontier*, ed. M. Darroll Bryant and Frank Flinn, New York: Paragon House 1989.

Paul Mojzes, '28 Guidelines for More Successful Dialogue' from 'The What and the How of Dialogue', *Inter-Religious Dialogue: Voices from a New Frontier*.

Raimon Panikkar, 'Rules of the Game in the Religious Encounter', *Intrareligious Dialogue*, New York: Paulist Press 1978.

World Council of Churches, *Guidelines on Dialogue with People of Living Faiths and Ideologies*, Geneva: World Council of Churches 1979.

Appendix 2

GUIDELINES FOR INTERRELIGIOUS UNDERSTANDING

Fr Thomas Keating OSCO, Convenor of the Snowmass Conference, 1984

Points of agreement or similarity between monastic representatives of religious traditions – Buddhist, Tibetan Buddhist, Hindu, Jewish, Islamic, Native American, Christian (Russian Orthodox, Protestant, Roman Catholic) – attending the Monastic Interfaith Dialogue.

1 The world religions bear witness to the experience of Ultimate Reality, to which they give various names: Brahman, Allah, Absolute, God, Great Spirit.

2 Ultimate Reality cannot be limited by any name or concept.

3 Ultimate Reality is the ground of infinite potentiality and actualization.

4 Faith is opening, accepting and responding to Ultimate Reality. Faith in this sense precedes every belief system.

5 The potential for human wholeness – or in other frames of reference, enlightenment, salvation, transformation, blessedness, *nirvana* – is present in every human person.

6 Ultimate Reality may be experienced not only through religious practices but also through nature, art, human relationships, and service of others.

7 As long as the human condition is experienced as separate from Ultimate Reality, it is subject to ignorance and illusion, weakness and suffering.

8 Disciplined practice is essential to the spiritual life; yet spiritual attainment is not the result of one's own efforts, but the result of the experience of oneness with Ultimate Reality.

Source: Thomas Keating, 'Theological Issues in Meditative Technologies', *Interfaith Spirituality, The Way Supplement* 78, Autumn 1993, p. 56.

Index of Names and Subjects